The 1922
St. Louis Browns

The 1922 St. Louis Browns

Best of the American League's Worst

Roger A. Godin

McFarland & Company, Inc., Publishers
Jefferson, North Carolina

The author is grateful to the *St. Louis Post-Dispatch* for permission to reprint poems by L. C. Davis (throughout book) and the statement by Dave Danforth (Appendix B).

The present work is a reprint of the library bound edition of The 1922 St. Louis Browns: Best of the American League's Worst, *first published in 1991 by McFarland.*

Library of Congress Cataloguing-in-Publication Data

Godin, Roger A., 1938–
The 1922 St. Louis Browns : best of the American League's worst / Roger A. Godin.
p. cm.
Includes bibliographical references and index.

ISBN 978-0-7864-7745-6
softcover : acid free paper ∞

1. St. Louis Browns (Baseball team)—History. I. Title.
GV875.S28G63 2014
796.357'64'0977866—dc20 90-53496

British Library cataloguing data are available

On the cover: St. Louis Browns first baseman George Sisler

Manufactured in the United States of America

McFarland & Company, Inc., Publishers
Box 611, Jefferson, North Carolina 28640
www.mcfarlandpub.com

IN MEMORIAM

PENNSYLVANIA MILITARY COLLEGE

1821–1972

Cave Anguis

CONTENTS

INTRODUCTION

I suspect that the origins of this book go back to the yellowed pages of a boyhood scrapbook. There, pasted to a page, are the boxscores of a doubleheader played sometime in 1947. The scores are 11–2 in the first game for Detroit over the home team St. Louis Browns, and another 10–1 romp for the Tigers in the nightcap.

For many those types of scores sum up the 52-year history of the St. Louis American League franchise. A history of futility marked by countless second division finishes and games like those immortalized in my scrapbook. And yet there is a fascination with such futility. Milton Richman, late UPI sports editor, reported receiving continued queries about the Browns more than 25 years after the team played its last game. William Mead's *Even the Browns,* an account of wartime baseball with emphasis on the Browns' 1944 pennant winners, appeared in 1978 to quite favorable reviews. Items of Browns memorabilia are eagerly fought after at premium prices, and the early 1980s saw a revival of the St. Louis Browns Fan Club under the able aegis of Bill Borst, the "Baseball Professor."

I confess that I, too, am caught up in this strange fascination. Originally I planned to write a complete team history, but the magnitude of that effort undertaken on a part-time basis simply seemed overwhelming. Then the thought occurred to me what swept people into this Browns mania was probably not the team's reputation as a chronic loser, but the rare occasions when the team rose to be a genuine contender. To put it another way, many of us, like the Browns, all too frequently fall short of our own expectations. But then we all have those relatively rare occasions when we are contenders in life's game. And what a joy those occasions are! Hence, a book concerning the Browns' 1944 pennant winners and the 1922 second place squad would probably hold some appeal. Since Bill Mead had already covered the 1944 team, I decided to write about the Browns of 1922.

Though few realize it, the 1922 St. Louis Browns were regarded by veteran baseball writer Tom Meaney as one of the sport's all time great teams and are so treated in that author's *Baseball's Greatest Teams,* which appeared in 1949. Consider the following about the 1922 club:

1. Fought the Yankees down to the wire for the American League flag, losing by only one game on the next to the last day of the season.

2. Led the American League in batting (.313), slugging (.455), runs (867), triples (94), stolen bases (132), walks (421), strikeouts (534), saves (22), and earned run average (3.38).

3. Six regulars – Jacobson, McManus, Severeid, Sisler, Tobin, and Williams – hit over .300. Jacobson, McManus, Sisler, and Williams all recorded more than 100 runs batted in, making the Browns the first team to have four or more such players in the starting lineup.

4. Collected seven extra base hits in the sixth inning of an August 7 game against Washington for the first time in the history of the American League. This post–1900 record was not tied until 1936 in the National League and 1940 in the American. The pre–1900 record is eight, held by the 1883 Chicago Cubs of the National League.

5. George Sisler led the league in batting (.420), runs (134), hits (246), triples (18), stolen bases (51), and assists (125), and had a 41-game hitting streak. He was named the American League's most valuable player.

6. Ken Williams led the league in home runs (39), runs batted

in (155), and total bases (367). In addition Williams, for the first time in the history of the American League, hit three home runs in one game against Chicago on April 22. This feat was part of a streak which saw the tall, slender, left-handed hitter belt out seven round-trippers in nine games between April 22 and 29. Later in the season Williams hit six circuit drives in six consecutive games between July 28 and August 2 and five four-baggers in five games during the September 4–9 time frame. On August 7 against Washington he became the first American League hitter to slug two home runs in one inning.

7. Urban Shocker led the league in strikeouts with 149.

8. Bill Bayne pitched a near no-hitter on May 5 against Detroit before allowing the Tigers a run and two hits in the ninth inning.

9. Bill Jacobson stroked out three triples against Detroit on September 9, a post–1900 record shared by a number of players. The pre–1900 record is four.

These are certainly not the statistics of a chronic loser! Nor is that designation entirely appropriate for the team's efforts through 1930. While certainly no world beaters, the Browns were generally competitive in their earlier years, particularly during the 1920s.

And so it was that this book came to be. Research began in earnest during 1978. I have had the benefit of being able to use the microfilm collections of the University of Minnesota's Wilson Library; University of Minnesota–Duluth Library; Hibbing, Minnesota Community College Library; New York Public Library; and Chicago Public Library. Newspapers primarily cited as sources are the *St. Louis Post-Dispatch, New York Times,* and the *Sporting News.*

No such undertaking as this can be accomplished without reference to those who participated in or were close to the participants in this epic year. Only a handful of team members were living when work began: Pruett, Bayne, Ellerbe, Robertson, and Billings. Pruett did not respond to my inquiry, and Bayne permitted only the use of quotes in a *St. Louis Globe Democrat* story, while both Robertson and Billings could not be located (I subsequently learned that both died in 1981). This left Frank "Governor" Ellerbe, the starting third baseman for the first half of the season, and he proved a gold mine of information, as readers will observe. My particular thanks to "Gov" and his sons, who assisted with the interview. It was with considerable sadness that I learned of "Gov's" passing in 1988.

Next of kin proved to be most helpful, and special thanks go to Mrs. Dorothy Tobin Brady, daughter of John Tobin; Mrs. Carita Johnson, daughter of Bill Jacobson; Mrs. Jane Weichlein, daughter of Hank Severeid; and Mr. James Tobin, brother of John Tobin. I must also single out the late Ray Gillespie, St. Louis baseball writer with the old *St. Louis Star*. Ray covered the Browns from 1923 onward, but was familiar with and saw the '22 team in action on numerous occasions. Ray's insights and helpfulness were most gratifying, and his passing in February 1979 left a real void among those who remember this golden year.

I would be remiss in not mentioning Bob Bauman, St. Louis Cardinal trainer and former Browns trainer (1938–1953), for his gracious assistance in leading me to both Mrs. Brady and Ray Gillespie. Others providing assistance were George Sisler, Jr.; Kenneth Vangilder, son of Elam Russell Vangilder; and my good friend Barry Fritz.

1

SPRING TRAINING

Alabamy Bound

"Mr. Ball, you are going to win a pennant *sure,*" said a baseball writer to the Browns' owner. The occasion was a celebration party in the magnate's room after the American Leaguers had defeated the Cardinals in a New Orleans exhibition game. Ball's spicily punctuated reply, tamed for publication, was: "I've listened to that bunky doodle for four years. I have a good club this year. The Cardinals are a mighty good club. Each has a chance. Do you understand, a chance. But for you to sit here on April 1 and tell me I'm going to win a pennant is silly. Boy, I've been of age for some time."

So reported J. Roy Stockton of the *St. Louis Post-Dispatch* on April 7, 1922. While Stockton didn't indicate if he was the writer in question, he did give us an insight into the turbulent personality that was Phillip DeCatesby Ball. Described as tough, austere, frank, and individualistic, Ball was the archtypical self-made man.

He was born in Keokuk, Iowa, on October 22, 1864. His strange middle name was the result of a compromise between his parents. His father wanted young Ball to carry as a middle name that of Ap Catesby, a famous Welshman. Mother Ball would have none of that, hence the compromise "DeCatesby."

Baseball proved to be Ball's passion, and he ultimately developed into a catcher. While with the Shreveport team he severely injured his left hand in a barroom knife fight, putting an end to any further baseball ambitions. But the future club owner had interests other than baseball. After working as a cowboy and on the railroad, he put together $1,000 and bought into an ice plant. The ex-catcher was on his way to becoming a millionaire.

The sport never left Ball's blood, and when he was financially able to do so he became actively involved by backing the St. Louis entry (along with Harry Sinclair of Tea Pot Dome scandal fame) in the new Federal League. The league folded in 1915 after two seasons, but American League President Ban Johnson gave Ball the opportunity to purchase the Browns in 1916. One of Ball's early accomplishments was assisting in working out an agreement whereby former Federal League players could return to the major leagues. Ball's 1916 Browns had twelve former St. Louis Federal League players on the roster.

By 1920 Ball and his general manager (then called business manager) Bob Quinn had formed the nucleus of a genuine contender. The greats who would form the core of the 1922 team were aboard: Sisler, Severeid, Tobin, Williams, Jacobson, Gerber, and Shocker. The club finished fourth in 1920 as Sisler hit .407 to lead the league and advanced to third the following year as Shocker won 27 games. The best was yet to come, despite Ball's protestations to the unfortunate writer of 1922.

Ray Gillespie, *St. Louis Star* baseball writer, remembered Phil Ball as

> a shrewd owner, knew the talent, but was tight fisted with a buck and didn't believe in overpaying his players. In fact he didn't feel they were entitled to the salaries he paid employees of his ice plant because the latter worked harder than the ball players. Ball was gruff with everybody, cursed and swore as part of his vocabulary, liked to win at any cost. He was known to travel to New York, Boston, Philadelphia to treat his entire roster of players to a stage production such as "No, No, Nanette" (financially backed by Boston Red Sox owner Harry Frazee).

Phillip DeCatesby Ball, the Browns' feisty owner, bought the team from Robert Hedges in 1916 and was still owner when he died in October 1933. (Photo courtesy of the *Sporting News*.)

Frederick Lieb, in his *The Baltimore Orioles: The History of a Colorful Team in Baltimore and St. Louis,* while agreeing with Gillespie on Ball's cantankerousness, said baseball monetary losses never bothered him. When his business manager, Bob Quinn, called off a game with Boston because of an early rain, Ball stormed into his office.

> "What's the reason for this? Why isn't there a game?" he demanded.
> "Oh, there were only a few hundred fans in the stands," hemmed and hawed Quinn. "A doubleheader later on will be more profitable."
> Ball shook his fist. "Bob Quinn, let me tell you something," he roared. "I worked myself to a frazzle at the office so I could see this game, and if you want to keep your job, don't ever do anything like this to me again."

While Ball was gruff and unpleasant there was another side to him as well. Dorothy Tobin Brady, daughter of right fielder John Tobin, recalls being told this story by her father:

> My dad was always a very light weight person. Phil Ball said to him at one time, "Johnny, you ought to get some meat on your bones." And my Dad said: "Oh, I've been light all my life." And he (Ball) said: "Do me a favor. When you go to bed at night have a good big sandwich and a bottle of beer. That will put meat on your bones." And by golly it did.

While Ball was clearly given to speaking his mind, his manager, Lee Fohl, was more the strong, silent type. Fohl was born in Marietta, Ohio, on November 28, 1876. His family soon moved to Pittsburgh, where he learned his baseball on the sandlots. He became a catcher and ultimately broke into organized baseball with Des Moines of the Western League. Appearing in only five major league games in his career, Fohl nonetheless became a solid minor leaguer with Columbus from 1905 to 1908. He got his first managing experience while still playing for Lima in the Ohio State League in 1909. He was playing manager for Akron of the Ohio-Penn League from 1910 to 1913.

Cleveland Naps (later Indians) owner Charley Somers took a liking to Fohl and signed him as playing manager of Cleveland's Waterbury, Connecticut, farm club in the Eastern League in 1914. After the Naps finished last that year, Somers brought Fohl up to replace Joe Birmingham as Cleveland bench manager in the middle of the 1915 season.

A good developer of players, Fohl brought the Cleveland club up to a seventh place finish in 1915, sixth in 1916, third in 1917, and a strong second in 1918. The next year was to be his undoing. Babe Ruth told it through Bob Considine in *The Babe Ruth Story:*

> Four of my 29 home runs that season (1919) were with the bases filled, and one of my grand slams did a good turn for my former Red Sox associate, Tris Speaker. It actually knocked Lee Fohl right off the managerial bench in Cleveland. The Indians were ahead when Fohl sent Fritz Coumbe, a former Red Sox member, to the mound as a relief pitcher with the bases filled. I knocked the ball over the right field screen at Cleveland's old League Park, giving the Red Sox the ball game. Jim Dunn, the Cleveland owner, got so sore at Fohl's pitching strategy that he fired Lee and put Tris Speaker in charge of the team.

The Indians finished in second place under Speaker and then went on to capture their first pennant and World Series victory in 1920. Fohl became a coach with the Browns in 1920 and then took over as manager in 1921. The team started slowly that year and on July 15 was in seventh place, only one and a half games ahead of the Philadelphia Athletics with a 35-48 record. Despite that performance, Fohl was rehired on July 17 for 1922, and no further incentive seemed to be needed. The team went 46-25 for the balance of the season, winding up third with an 81-73 slate. By finishing third the Browns were assured of a part of the World Series money.

Gillespie on Fohl: "I always felt that Lee Fohl was an excellent manager, knew baseball thoroughly, but was often second-guessed by his players because there was never much rapport between him and his men. He had an odd personality, seemingly hard to understand and not easy to get along with."

Frank "Governor" Ellerbe, the Browns' regular third baseman for the first part of the 1922 season, offered another view of Fohl: "He was a fine old man, but hardly as smart as the two other managers I played under, Clark Griffith and Tris Speaker. He wasn't as quick on the trigger, wasn't as smart."

Coming out of 1921 both Fohl and Quinn felt that the acquisition of an additional pitcher would make the team a genuine contender. While second and third base were regarded as real problems in the early stages of 1921, the development of rookie Marty McManus at second base and the acquisition of Frank Ellerbe from Washington for third base solved these problems. It was generally felt that the failure of the pitching staff hurt the team's chances.

Urban Shocker, the veteran spitballer, was the staff ace. In 1921 he had won 27 games against 12 losses, placing him second behind the Yankees' Carl Mays in pitching victories. At one point he reeled off eight wins in a row. Once past Shocker, however, the ranks grew thin. Frank "Dixie" Davis finished with 16-16 after an outstanding 18-12 record in 1920. Righthander Elam Vangilder was only 11-12, though he and lefthander Billy Bayne, 11-5, pitched well in the later stages of the 1921 season.

As the annual minor league meetings approached in December 1921, the *Sporting News* observed:

> Bob Quinn ... figures that the pitching he must have—and the Browns need little else—is likely to come from the higher class minors.... The Browns are in good shape to make deals, for they have surplus infield and outfield talent that the minor league moguls pine for. They can trade a couple of fielders and throw in a second rate pitcher for a minor league twirling star, of whom there are several not yet sold for spring delivery.

One who was apparently ready for spring delivery was southpaw Dave Danforth. Danforth, who had seen prior major league service with the Chicago White Sox, had compiled a 25-15 record with the last place Columbus club of the American Association. The record is particularly remarkable in light of the fact that Columbus won only 67 games, making Danforth responsible for better than a third of the team's victories. He had struck out 201 batters and walked only 113 in 320 innings.

With such impressive statistics it is not surprising that the price for him was high. Quinn gave up eight players, but none who were considered regulars. Only relief pitchers Bill Burwell and Emilio Palmero as well as reserve infielder Dudly Lee had spent the entire prior season with the Browns.

The deal, which was completed on December 14 at Buffalo, N.Y., where the minor league meetings were being held, was hailed in St. Louis. The *Sporting News* was especially estatic:

> The Browns have the pitching, no team in their league has anything better, and they should be able to start with it in the beginning as Fohl promises. With pitching the Browns have about everything. What club has a better infield? A better outfield? A better coaching staff? All those enumerated and included have to do is get up and get going at the same gait they set last year. The first string men have quality and the reserve forces have qualifications. The slogan of the Browns should be and must be from now on "Let's go."

Optimism proved so rampant that a long-standing St. Louis tradition – the city series with the tenant Cardinals (Phil Ball also owned Sportsman's Park) – was threatened. Starting in 1903, one year after the Browns' entry into the American League, the two St. Louis entries in the major leagues had engaged in both spring and fall series to determine the city champion. While the fall series was discontinued after 1917, the spring games, which were best-four-of-seven affairs, were eagerly awaited by the Mound City population as a prelude to another major league season. Evidence of the enthusiasm for these games can be seen by the fact that more than 74,000 fans attended the seven games in 1921. The Browns won four games to three, and both teams divided gate receipts of about $60,000.

In early January 1922 it was announced, following conferences between Ball and Quinn for the Browns and Branch Rickey and Sam Beardon of the Cardinals, that the normal best-four-of-seven series would be abandoned. Only two games, scheduled for Saturday and Sunday, April 8 and 9, would be played, though the possibility of spring training games in the South was not ruled out. As things developed two more games were played in New Orleans in April 1 and 2.

What brought about this sudden change in an old tradition? Pennant fever is the only answer. The *Post-Dispatch* quoted Bob Quinn solemnly intoning:

> Both clubs, we figure, have a chance for the pennant next season (1922), and we will not put the added worry of a spring series on the players' minds in an effort to get off on the right foot in the league races. Many fans have told us that we are passing up a lot of money by calling off the spring series, but money is not everything in baseball. Anyway, we are going to abandon the spring series as a tryout for 1922.

In backing up their decision to abandon, or more properly, reduce the scope of the spring series, club officials cited the poor starts of both teams in 1921. The season began on April 13, and one month later the Browns were in sixth place with a record of 10-13 while the Cardinals were 5-15 and in last place at the end of April.

With the city series "problem" thus disposed of, a legitimate concern came to the forefront: the selection of a spring training site. The Browns had trained at Bogalusa, Louisiana, in 1921, but the bungalows used to house the players were no longer available. The lumber company that was the principal industry of the town had sold this housing to their employees, leaving only one inadequate hotel to billet the team. The exhibition schedule had by this time, mid–January, been drawn up to the extent that dates in New Orleans and Pensacola, Florida, were included, making the selection of another nearby location imperative.

Quinn was dispatched to the South to find a suitable location. He was not long in determining that Mobile, Alabama, would be the ideal spot. Meeting with President Robert Weinacker of the Mobile club of the Southern Association, Quinn quickly made the necessary arrangements to use Mobile's Monroe Park and the

The Battle House Hotel, Mobile, Alabama: The spring training home of the 1922 St. Louis Browns. (Photo courtesy of the Museum of the City of Mobile.)

lodging facilities of the Battle House Hotel. Mobile had hosted the Louisville Colonels of the American Association the two prior springs, so the community was not new to baseball spring training, though the Browns would be their first major league club. The move brought this optimistic response from L. C. Davis, the *Post-Dispatch's* resident sports poet: "The Browns will leave Bogalusa flat on her back this spring and train in Mobile. The further south they go the higher up they finish."

On January 18 the preliminary exhibition schedule was released: March 11, 12, 15, 18, 19, and 22, Mobile at Mobile; March 25, 26, 27, Louisville at Pensacola; March 28, 29, New Orleans at New Orleans; March 30, 31, St. Paul at New Orleans; April 1, 2, Cardinals at New Orleans; April 3, 4, 5, 6, to be announced. President Jules Heineman of the New Orleans club had made six dates available at his ball park, allowing the Browns and Cardinals to stage part of the abbreviated city series on neutral territory.

The compactness of the schedule will be noted. Pensacola was but a brief three hours from Mobile and New Orleans only five. As Quinn told the *Sporting News*:

> Our idea of exhibition games during spring training is to get as many of them right together as possible and avoid the one night jumps. We do not feel that any club can get into condition riding on sleepers [trains] every night. After all it is not a question of how much money you can get on exhibition games, the chief consideration is how much good practice you can get to put your club in condition.

As January turned to February the baseball news began to pick up. On February 2 the *Post-Dispatch* reported that manager Lee Fohl would take only 29 players to Mobile for spring training, the smallest in many seasons. This 29 included pitchers Urban Shocker, Frank "Dixie" Davis, Elam Vangilder, Bill Bayne, Dave Danforth, Ray "Jockey" Kolp, Wayne "Rasty" Wright, Jim Elliot, Henry Meine, Frank Henry, Frank Halliday, and Henry Deine; catchers Hank Severeid, Josh Billings, Pat Collins, John Heving, and Arthur Watkins; infielders George Sisler, Marty McManus, Wally Gerber, Gene Robertson, Jimmy Austin, Frank Ellerbe, and Bill Mullen; and outfielders Johnny Tobin, Ken Williams, William "Baby Doll" Jacobson, Chick Shorten, and Cedric Durst.

The next day the complete exhibition schedule was released indicating the following additional games: April 3, Meridian (Cotton States League) at Meridian, Mississippi; April 4, Clinton College at Vicksburg, Miss.; April 5, Jackson (Cotton States League) at Jackson, Miss.; April 6, Minneapolis (American Association) at

Dyersburg, Tennessee. The schedule would conclude with the two previously announced games with the Cardinals at Sportsman's Park.

Quinn spent some time denying that certain players might not be with the club any longer and that others were unhappy. Press reports out of Boston indicated that Jimmy Austin, the team's oldest veteran and coach, was finished with the Browns. Not true, said the Browns' business manager. Austin was under contract. Nor was Urban Shocker unhappy with the club despite rumors to the contrary. On the latter Quinn said: "Not so (unhappy). We need him. With another like him we'd win the championship. Even as we stand we've got a good chance."

Signed contracts were received from Gerber, McManus, and Ellerbe to go with those of Austin, Mullen, Robertson, Shorten, Danforth, Sisler, Shocker, Tobin, and Severeid. The latter four were serving the second year of two-year pacts.

The fact that there were players with two-year contracts is of particular interest in view of the *Sporting News* story of February 15 headlined "Browns May Dump a Pair of Ingrates." The article went on at some length concerning the efforts of two unidentified players to, in the parlance of today, renegotiate their contracts. What has become a common practice in today's baseball was regarded as heresy in 1922:

> They wanted the contracts they thought so good a year previous cancelled and the new ones at higher figures entered into. They were tickled to death to sign for long terms before, but because they got a few extra hits or something during the year they straightaway concluded they were in a position to play both ends against the middle and do the neat little stand and deliver act. Quinn, it is reported, told them to go jump. . . .

The first trek south to Mobile began on February 14 when Urban Shocker left to join minor leaguer Bill Mullen, already in the Alabama city. Lee Fohl arrived in St. Louis from his Cleveland home on February 18 and departed with the batterymen on

February 22 on the 24-hour train ride to Mobile. Rain greeted the advance party on the 23rd, but it soon cleared and the remainder of the week was ideal for training.

Fohl launched into a vigorous training routine according to the *Sporting News*. Prior to departure both Fohl and Quinn were concerned that the Mardi Gras season then in full swing might adversely affect training. President Weinacker of the host Mobile club had urged the players to bring along dress suits as he would issue cards allowing admission to all the various activities. Intent that the holiday atmosphere would not undermine his plans, Fohl "compelled his men to be out four or five hours a day. The weary athletes, though invited to the nightly balls, have posed as wall flowers, too fagged to fox trot or shimmy." Fohl did relent on February 28, when the *Post-Dispatch* indicated that the players went to the wharf for the masked ball, the final session of the Mardi Gras activities.

The later part of February saw the signed contracts of Williams, Wright, and Davis arrive at the Browns' offices. But there remained a major problem with Dave Danforth. The veteran southpaw refused to report until the Columbus team agreed to a settlement with him. The settlement was based on Danforth's contention that Columbus had originally agreed to give him a percentage of whatever he should bring if sold. The Texas native felt that 10 percent of the cash value of the eight players dealt to the American Association club would be adequate compensation. Quinn was ultimately forced to get involved along with American League President Ban Johnson. The matter was finally resolved to Danforth's satisfaction, but it appears doubtful that he collected the $10,000 he was rumored to be seeking.

Shortly after Fohl and the batterymen's arrival in Mobile, the Browns and all of baseball were shocked by the sudden death of Cardinals catcher Bill "Pickles" Dillhoefer. The National League club's reserve receiver had contracted typhoid fever five days after marrying and succumbed on February 22. Dillhoefer's wife was a Mobile native, and he was buried there on the 25th. The Browns attended the funeral as a group.

Intrasquad games were featured in the early days of spring training as Fohl sought to find one more pitcher who would insure a balanced, winning staff. It was thought that Dave Danforth would be that pitcher, but he had yet to report. Another serious possibility was Wayne Wright, who was returning to the Browns after two years with the American Association Louisville Colonels. He, too, had not arrived in Mobile. The veteran pitchers in camp complained of stiffness and soreness after their initial workouts. Elam Vangilder expressed his desire for a fast start as quoted in the *Post-Dispatch*:

> I haven't accomplished much since joining the Browns for the reason that I could never get off to a good start. Last year it was late in the season before I got going real well, and then I showed the boys something. I want to jump right in when the bell rings this spring and be up among the leaders when the Browns finish at home next October. And I am going to be up there.

Fohl was particularly hopeful that rookie Roy Davis might develop, but after an initial favorable impression he was hit hard in subsequent games. In an 8–8 intrasquad game tie on February 26, Coach "Lefty" Leifield tagged the young hurler for a three-run homer.

The weather turned bad thereafter, curtailing games, but Fohl continued to work the squad in the outfield areas of Monroe Park through shagging flies, bunting games, and running laps. Starting March 1 the veteran "name" players began to arrive on the scene. One of the foremost of these was outfielder Ken Williams, who was to enjoy the most successful season of his career in 1922. Williams had collected 25 home runs in 1921, and his first day in camp he knocked five over the fence, prompting the *Post-Dispatch* to observe:

> Strange thing about Williams is that whenever he reports in town for spring training work, dons his uniform and begins hitting, it always follows that several boards in the

> right field fence are immediately taken off. It's a tough job climbing the fence to retrieve baseballs, and for this reason those players stationed in right field endeavor to make the task as easy as possible.

The weather then turned cold and wet, precluding any work for two days as the players relaxed at the Battle House. By March 4 Gerber, Ellerbe, Shorten, Jacobson, and Robertson had arrived, leaving only George Sisler and Johnny Tobin among the regulars still due in. Both had permission for late arrival, with Sisler's children being ill and Tobin celebrating his eighth wedding anniversary on March 4.

Workouts resumed on the 4th with rookie outfielder Cedric Durst being particularly impressive. Durst was a discovery of former Browns first baseman Pat Newman and had spent the 1921 season with Beaumont of the Texas League. Though hitting only a rather average .274 the Browns front office was quite high on Durst. Newman felt he was the most outstanding young defensive outfielder he had ever seen, while Quinn wondered aloud how he could be kept out of the starting line up. Durst impressed enough to remain with the team for the entire season, but came to bat only twelve times and never did succeed in establishing himself as a regular in the major leagues.

On the morning of the 4th Fohl provided some relief from the training camp routine when the Browns were the guests of James R. Lyons, the Collector of the Port, on the revenue cutter *Messenger* for a trip on the Mobile River. The *Post-Dispatch* reported that British ambassador Sir Auckland Geddes was aboard with a group of friends, but apparently felt the presence of the Browns made things a bit too crowded for comfort and departed for another vessel. Hardly a diplomatic move for an ambassador! No doubt Fohl hoped that the boat ride would provide some type of diversion for the players as Mobile's racing season was about to begin. The city's hotels were filled with owners, jockeys, and bookmakers, while another segment of the population was looking forward to the opening of a professional golf tournament.

On March 6 Lee Fohl greeted George Sisler and Johnny

Tobin's arrival at camp and may have first realized that his search for another might soon bear fruit. Pat Collins and Jimmy Austin led the youngsters – or yannigans, as the reserves were commonly called – to a 6–4 victory over the regulars. Six pitchers were used in the game, with a young medical student from the University of Missouri, Hubert "Shucks" Pruett, working the last three innings for the youngsters and showing good speed and control. The lefthanded Pruett had stepped off the Missouri campus the prior June and joined the Tulsa club of the Western League. He was sufficiently impressive there to earn an invitation to the Browns' 1922 camp. The year was to prove his most successful major league season and earn him a niche in baseball history unfilled by any other pitcher.

With Sisler and Tobin in camp, Fohl had now assembled the lineup that he intended to use over the 21-game exhibition schedule beginning on Saturday, March 11. Neither player showed any effects from the off-season break (Sisler had played winter ball in California), and both hit well in their first workout. Sisler knocked three balls over the fence and Tobin two as high winds precluded an intrasquad game, but apparently aided the long ball hitting. The two men participated in a 4–0 victory for the regulars over the yannigans the following day, March 8, although Pruett threw three innings of no-hit ball for the newcomers. The Browns reinforced their bench by signing Herman Bronkie, former Mobile manager and second baseman.

On March 9 Dave Danforth finally arrived in camp, claiming illness in the family for his late arrival, but the controversey over the settlement he should receive was the more likely reason for his tardiness. Danforth was optimistic about the Browns' pennant chances, indicating that he thought the Yankees would have difficulty repeating. The day's intrasquad game featured Urban Shocker's debut as the regulars laced the yannigans 11–3. Shocker scattered six hits and gave up two runs in five innings, while Vangilder surrendered four hits and one run over the last four innings.

The eve of the exhibition season was now at hand, and the

veteran members of the team assembled in the clubhouse and set as their objective victory in all 21 exhibition games. Fohl sent the pitchers through a lengthy session of fielding bunts while the remainder of the squad engaged in bunting games and tossing around the medicine ball. Fohl announced the starting lineup for the first game against Mobile:

Tobin rf
Ellerbe 3b
Sisler 1b
Williams lf
Jacobson cf
Severeid c
Gerber ss
McManus 2b
Vangilder and
Bayne p

This was the same group that had closed the season the prior October against Detroit, with the exception of Williams, who had sat out the Tiger series with a bad knee. This same lineup, with the exception of Ellerbe, who would go out with a July injury, would see the Browns rise to their finest heights.

Mobile kept it close for eight innings in the inaugural spring game, but a six-run outburst in the ninth settled the issue for the Browns. Leading 5–4, St. Louis batted around the four singles, two walks, two errors, and three stolen bases, bringing in six runs. One of the stolen bases was George Sisler's theft of home plate. Fohl worked Roy Davis into the game, but he gave up two of Mobile's runs on a seventh inning home run. Meanwhile, Pruett, the apparent sleeper of the new pitchers, retired the home team on eleven pitches in the ninth.

The little lefthander was back the next day as Mobile extended the Browns to ten innings before Wally Gerber tallied the winning run on Johnny Tobin's infield out. Relieving in the eighth Pruett allowed only two hits and one walk over the last three innings. Both Williams and Sisler hit solo home runs as the Browns had difficulty with Mobile pitchers Sigman and Fulton.

Fohl put the club through workouts the next two days as Dave Danforth exercised for the first time and indicated he would be ready to pitch the following Saturday if nominated. Business manager Quinn arrived on the 14th and pronounced himself well satisfied with the club's progress. The practice that day was confined to batting and fielding, and eight pitchers were used. The *Post-Dispatch's* correspondent was particularly impressed with Vangilder and Severeid:

> [Vangilder] sent the leather over the plate with plenty of stuff behind each offering and his control was excellent. Vangilder looks better this spring than ever before.... Hank Severeid is now hitting the ball in his old style, sending drives to left field. Hank takes a mighty smash at the leather when he swings and judging from the way he has been connecting, the veteran catcher is due to be right up there with the swat leaders.

Resuming exhibition play on March 15, the Browns easily defeated Mobile 7–3 as the minor leaguers made eight errors and Johnny Tobin went three for three. Fohl pulled the regulars after four innings, leaving only Gerber and McManus in the game. He again used Roy Davis, but Mobile got their three runs off him aided by two errors.

Observing that Fohl had used rookies Gene Robertson and Bill Mullen at shortstop and third base for parts of the Mobile games, the *Sporting News* commented: "Ellerbe and Gerber might as well know that if they mean to be regulars this year they have to win the honor on merit, for Robertson and Mullen are just as much members of the team as the older men."

Commenting on Marty McManus, the baseball weekly included a use of the vernacular surprising to even today's regulars: "This boy need only continue the improvement he was showing in 1921 to hold his job against all comers. He showed last year he found himself, after a bad start, and it will be an upset to the dope if he doesn't establish himself as a star."

It was apparent that some of the Browns were enjoying

themselves off the field as well as on. The *Post-Dispatch's* L. C. Davis observed: "A number of Browns cashed in on the last race at Mobile the other day. Looks like first division."

The club spent March 16 and 17 in normal workouts with an intrasquad game on the 17th. Once again the regulars walloped the yannigans by a one-sided 10–2 count; once again, Pruett impressed and Davis did not. This time Pruett worked for the regulars and gave up one hit in three innings, though two runs scored as the result of three errors. Davis was pounded by the regulars for four runs on four hits, two walks, and an error.

The series with Mobile resumed on the weekend of March 18–19 and resulted in two more Browns victories. On Saturday a seven-run fourth inning won the game early, though the minor leaguers continued to chip away in later innings before succumbing 8–5. While Jacobson and Williams homered, Mobile had the play of the game when they executed a triple play in the eighth inning. McManus led off with a single off Sigman, who had given the Browns trouble the previous weekend. Henry Meine, the St. Louis pitcher, reached first on an infield hit, McManus going to second. Tobin then lined to Leathers at shortstop who tossed to Niehoff at second, retiring McManus. Niehoff then threw to Huhn at first to get Meine. Despite the success that St. Louis would have in 1922 it was a play they would not execute themselves.

Sunday marked the long-awaited debut of Dave Danforth. While the Browns toyed with Mobile 14–5, the former White Sox hurler gave up all five runs on eight hits. While Fohl might have been disappointed, he could have not been more encouraged by Shocker's two-hit, three-inning stint. There was speculation that the veteran spitballer was ready for a more lengthy stint. Most of the regulars were replaced in the fifth inning, but not before George Sisler inspired the crowd with a three-run home run in the second inning.

Inspiration was something that George Sisler could manage quite easily, as we will observe in the pages ahead. But an incident during spring training, later related by *Post-Dispatch* sports editor John Wray, reflected on Sisler the man:

> George was standing in the lobby of the Battle House when he heard the boys [visitors from northern Alabama] whispering to an old man asking him if we would point out Sisler. George went over to the boys and introduced himself and spent half an hour chatting with them about baseball and their homes. Then George took the boys under his care and introduced them to Lee Fohl, Kenny Williams, Johnny Tobin and every other Brown who could be found.
>
> That afternoon the boys were George's guests at the ball park. When they went back home that night they were ready to lay down their lives for George Sisler.
>
> A newspaper writer told George how much he admired him for having treated the boys that way.
>
> George blushed. "Say, I wouldn't hurt a kid's feelings for the world. I was a kid myself. It must hurt to have someone you admire snub you or hurt your feelings. Those kids came all the way to Mobile to see some ball players. And I would have cut off my right hand before I'd let them be disappointed."

As the spring training period entered its fourth full week the Browns could look forward to the visit of the commissioner of baseball, Judge Kennesaw Mountain Landis, on March 20 and the breaking of camp on March 24. The story of Landis's installation as baseball czar following the infamous Black Sox scandal of 1919 is well known and needs no retelling here. Suffice it to say the Judge was a follower of the straight and narrow, and nothing is more indicative of his character than his deportment while playing golf. Later in the week while on the course with Jimmy Austin and "Lefty" Leifield, he hit into a thicket of saplings. Austin bent one of the trees out of his way. The *Post-Dispatch* reported the Judge's response: "No, we can't do that, Mr. Jimmy. We got to play 'em as they are in this game. Just stand aside and listen to me swear if that tree bothers me." We can probably assume that there was some swearing as Landis finished the 18 holes with a 120!

Landis had been greeted on his arrival in Mobile by just about every V.I.P. in the city: the mayor and city commissioners, Bob Quinn, President Weinacker of the Mobile club, and numerous other town notables. Later in the evening he was entertained at a banquet by the local automobile club. After the previously described golf match, the following day the commissioner watched the Browns destroy Springhill College 16–5 at the college campus.

After the Judge's departure the Browns resumed their assault on Mobile on March 22 with a 9–1 romp as Sisler went five for five including a home run. In a prophetic comment, the *Post-Dispatch*'s J. Roy Stockton, who had just arrived from the Cardinal's camp, noted: "He [Sisler] would have had a triple on one of his doubles, but Bronkie was ahead of him and George almost ran over him rounding the sacks. He [Bronkie] won't get in there this season unless Ellerbe goes blind or is injured."

The only major league club that the Browns were scheduled to face in the spring was the Cardinals at New Orleans and St. Louis. Now a quirk permitted a game against the National League Brooklyn Dodgers. Originally scheduled to oppose Mobile on March 23, the Dodgers were rescheduled against the Browns. The game proved to be a sterner test than the most recent outings of Fohl's players.

Bob Quinn departed for St. Louis prior to this game and thereby missed Urban Shocker's five-inning, two-hit shutout effort and Bill Bayne's four-inning, two-hit, two-run completion. The Browns won 4–2. The McManus-Gerber combination at second base and shortstop looked impressive, as did Ellerbe at third base. Sisler was finally challenged by major league pitching as he went hitless on the day, including a rare called strike three thrown by Brooklyn's Dazzy Vance.

The time at Mobile was now drawing to an end for most of the club's personnel. Fohl announced that the following would make the trip to Pensacola for a three-game series with Louisville of the American Association March 25–27: pitchers Urban Shocker, Elam Vangilder, Bill Bayne, Frank Davis, Dave Danforth, Wayne Wright, Ray Kolp, Hubert Pruett, and Frank Henry; catchers Hank Severeid, Pat Collins, and Arthur Watkins; infielders George Sisler, Wally Gerber, Frank Ellerbe, Marty

McManus, Jimmy Austin, and Gene Robertson; outfielders Johnny Tobin, Ken Williams, and Bill Jacobson.

The remainder of the squad was to remain in Mobile and continue to oppose the minor league entry with games on March 25 and 26. Among those left back, outfielders Chick Shorten and rookie Cedric Durst as well as catcher Josh Billings were regarded as almost certain to make the final roster. That left one more slot available, which knowledgeable observers felt should go to the recently acquired Herman Bronkie.

If there was earlier concern that Fohl would run too tight a spring training routine, it was apparent by this time that his modus operandi was exactly the opposite. The *Post-Dispatch*'s Stockton observed: "Discipline is a word never heard in the Browns' camp. There are no rules, not one, and the only men who abuse that fact are men who would not be bound by rules anyhow. There is no curfew, no calling in the morning, no anti-gambling rules, none against smoking and apparently the behavior of everyone is first class."

Not only was the behavior of everyone first class, so was the physical condition of the team, particularly the pitchers, as they headed for Pensacola. Fohl told Stockton:

> There is not a sore arm on the squad. All the pitchers are ready right now to start the season, if it were necessary. I am a firm believer in the wisdom of having one workout a day and have been very careful in that one session a day to see that the pitchers did not get too much. There has been no rubbing of arms because none was needed. The amount of work in that session was increased gradually and my pitchers now testify to the wisdom of the course pursued.

Urban Shocker had his own thoughts on conditioning, which he shared with Stockton:

> I came down to Mobile a week before the squad, but I did not start training until the first group arrived February 23.

> In other years, I directed my first attention to getting my body into condition. I worked hard to harden myself and paid virtually no attention to my arm until well along in the training period. This year I began with my arm and virtually spent all my time getting it into condition. I began by throwing the ball around, just tossing it for several days before I even started to throw any distance. I found that 100 throws, just light tosses, hardened my arm and prepared it best for the strain of pitching. I would work until my muscles were good and tired, but I never put any great effort into one pitch. The result was that my arm hardened gradually and there never was a chance to get the arm sore.
>
> I never passed up a chance to work the arm, but even when it came to the practice games, I put no speed into my pitching, merely experimenting with control. Why when I pitched against Brooklyn Thursday, I just threw them in places where the ball would be hard to hit. That is the big thing in pitching.

Fohl's penchant for a closed mouth was never more evident than at Mobile, according to Stockton: "Veterans of the team tell you Fohl never gives the players a word of advice, praise or criticism.... If you want to know what Fohl thinks it's best to happen to be near when he is planning with 'Lefty' Leifield or some other lieutenant. Then his conversation shows he sees just as much and forms opinions just as sharply as those of Rickey (Branch)."

And so it was on to Pensacola, where the playing field left much to be desired. It was literally a sandlot. Balls not caught by the outfielders would drop dead much like a golf ball hitting a bunker, while the fielders would slip and slide attempting to make putouts. The infield, around the bases, on the mound, and near the plate, was covered with clay. Despite the conditions, Fohl's athletes slammed out 18 hits in a 16–11 triumph as Sisler had another five for five day including a home run. Johnny Tobin returned to the lineup after missing the Brooklyn game because of indigestion and picked up two hits. Vangilder, Pruett, and Kolp worked parts of the game, and while Pruett gave up three hits and four runs in his two-inning stint, the playing field was responsible for two of the hits.

The March 26 game was rained out, but the Browns won again on the 27th 6–3. Dave Danforth hurled the last three innings, giving up two runs on three hits and striking out six. Danforth had a tricky move to first base that many thought was a balk. Stockton commented: "It is impossible to tell whether Danforth is about to throw to first or the plate. He starts with the same windup, kicks with his right foot in either case and as he throws he steps either toward first or toward the plate."

Fohl felt there was no reason for concern. He told Stockton: "I've heard that a dozen times and I want to tell you that it is ridiculous. If a pitcher has a motion that is illegal some umpire will call him for it and the motion will be discontinued. And a balk is not a balk until an umpire calls it a balk."

Jacobson was the hitting star with a home run and a triple, while "Dixie" Davis, who frequently had control problems, walked no one in five innings and scattered four hits.

While the Browns were delighted to be gone from Pensacola and its miserable playing field, they were greeted by another problem in New Orleans. They arrived early on the 28th to oppose New Orleans of the Southern Association, but rain began to fall en route, causing the game to be postponed and forcing the club to check into its hotel early. This proved impossible because of the checkout time, and the result was that most of the players sat around on the stairways waiting for their room assignments to become available. Some were still without accommodations as late as 6 p.m.

This inconvenience, while annoying, gave them plenty of time for conversation. Speculation about the coming pennant race included comments which sound as if they could have been uttered in the late 1970s in reference to George Steinbrenner's New York Yankees. The *Post-Dispatch*'s Stockton noted: "There is a strong tendency to pass up the Yankees as far as first place is concerned. Everybody respects Babe Ruth and his slugging buddies and it is granted that the club will be hard to beat. But there is a deep-rooted impression that there are too many tempermental prima donnas on the Yankee roster and that if the team ever has a little slump the Yanks will not be speaking to each other."

But all was not serious conversation in the hotel lobby. There was time for mathematical calculations as described by Stockton:

> John (Tobin) wants to know how fast a string of ball players stationed at intervals all the way, could relay a baseball from St. Louis to Chicago. He wanted to wager any part of a dime that the players – if they were all outfielders – could get the ball to its destination ahead of a fast train. Maxie Gerber grabbed a pencil and figured out the meal money it would take and concluded wistfully it would never be tried.

The day's inactivity had no adverse effect on the players, as they went out the following day and destroyed New Orleans 11–0. Shocker pitched hitless ball for five innings, giving away to Bill Bayne in the sixth inning. The only two balls hit out of the infield for New Orleans were two singles surrendered by Bayne. Gerber sparkled at shortstop, ranging far and wide in both directions.

While the Browns were becoming restless facing minor league opposition, they showed no mercy. St. Paul of the American Association fell 6–0 and 16–6 on March 30 and 31st. "Dixie" Davis, Dave Danforth, and Wayne Wright each pitched three scoreless innings as Jacobson homered in the 6–0 game. The 16–6 waltz was victory number 13 in a row as Sisler homered once again and Pruett continued to impress with three shutout, hitless innings.

But now the true test awaited the club. Despite all the protestations of Quinn and Fohl about the adverse effects of the city series, it was evident that the games with the Cardinals were the only real opposition to be faced before the regular season began and were to be fought with just as much intensity as in prior years regardless of venue. Stockton reflects this intensity:

> Shocker will pitch and he is as fit as they make them. Not a regular is ailing. Infield and outfield is eager for the fight and if the Rickeymen [Cardinals] win they will deserve all the praise that can be bestowed on them. Except for the hardened muscles and sharpened batting eyes that will come as the season progresses, the Browns will take the field tomorrow in as fine a playing condition as they can hope to attain this season.

Pointing up further the importance of the games was the arrival of Phil Ball, along with his partner and team vice president Walter Fritsch, for the series. Fritsch had been visiting other American League training camps to evaluate the opposition, and he joined Ball in New Orleans for the St. Paul series as well.

Fohl let Shocker go the full route on April 1 for the first such effort of the spring. His mound opponent was lefthander Bill Sherdel, who also went the distance. Shocker gave up nine hits and Sherdel a dozen; the outcome was not decided until the bottom of the ninth. With the score tied 5–5 Gerber led off the ninth with a single to center. McManus was safe on the attempted sacrifice when Sherdel hesitated before making the throw to first. That brought Shocker up, and on the attempted sacrifice Sherdel threw Gerber out at third. The Browns protested vigously to umpire Schaefer, but it mattered little when Johnny Tobin stroked a single over Cardinal second baseman Rogers Hornsby to score McManus from second with the winning run. Earlier Ken Williams had showed his disdain for lefthanded pitching by getting the game's only home run with Severeid aboard in the sixth.

But the club's apparent mid-season form and winning streak of fourteen came to an end as they booted away the April 2 game with five errors. Though the Browns sported a comfortable 6–2 lead going into the seventh inning, errors both official and unofficial allowed the Cardinals to score three runs. Vangilder had relieved starter "Dixie" Davis in the sixth when the latter had given up a run on three walks and a single. If the support behind him had been better, Vangilder might have picked up the victory. With one out in the seventh Gerber fumbled Fournier's grounder, but the official scorer generously ruled it a hit. Milton Stock then walked, bringing future Hall of Famer Hornsby to the plate. He hit an easy fly to right field which Tobin simply dropped, loading the bases. Mueller then grounded out, allowing Fournier to score. McHenry followed by singling in both Stock and Hornsby to cut the once solid lead to 6–5. While the Cardinals did not score again in the seventh, the Browns' infield play continued to deteriorate. Gerber booted Toporcer's roller, but escaped without an official error being charged. Frank Ellerbe was not so lucky. He was charged with an error for bobbling Ainsworth's grounder, which loaded the bases. Fortunately pinch hitter Burt Shotten was used, bringing this observation from the *Post-Dispatch*: "Traveling through the bushes is not what one would call real sport."

No travel was needed after this game as the next opponent was Jackson of the Cotton States League. Earlier in the spring, Clint Abrams, a Ball confident and friend, had purchased the team with two other Jackson residents. Accordingly the Browns themselves as well as their other farm clubs at Mobile and Terra Haute, Indiana, were expected to provide player help. Should all not go well in Jackson the *Sporting News* felt the players would have no worries:

> Ball players could do no worse than work for Clint Abrams. If the Cotton States League blows up they will be sure of jobs picking cotton or currying mules on his nearby plantation.... And if they are handy around the camp they can win permanent homes, for the Abrams plantation calls for many activities, ranging from bedding down the hogs to keeping at bay the phantom bear that threatens the Abrams' poultry pen o' nights.

Perhaps some of the Jackson players were ready for the hogs after the Browns got through with them on April 5. The result was a 14–1 rout as Vangilder and Wright shared the pitching chores. The one Jackson run came on, of all things, a rare steal of home in the ninth.

The Browns moved on to Dyersburg, Tennessee, the next

day, where St. Joseph of the Western League replaced the American Association Minneapolis Millers as the opposition. The game was somewhat more of a challenge as the Browns won 9–4, pounding out twelve hits to go into St. Louis with an 18–1 record. Though impressive on paper, the squad was only 2–1 against major league opposition and had been seriously challenged by minor league teams in only a handful of games. While the team exuded confidence, it was evident that a sweep of the Cardinals in the last two spring training games was essential to establish the Browns' credibility as a genuine contender.

Fohl worked the team at Sportsman's Park the morning of April 6 and indicated that Urban Shocker would again oppose the Cardinals on Saturday. Fohl expressed satisfaction that everyone was healthy and there were no sore arms among the pitchers. The latter condition had been attributed to "Dixie" Davis, but his problem was now described as a normal "kink" to be expected after a workout.

St. Louis was rampant with baseball fever as the final two games of the abbreviated city series got underway, though early morning rain held the crowd down to 12,000. The Cardinals repeated with pitcher Bill Sherdel for the Saturday game. The contest proved to be a near replica of the earlier game staged at New Orleans exactly one week before. With the score tied 2–2 going into the ninth, Jacobson led off with a single over second. Sherdel got Severeid to pop up, but then gave up a single to Ken Williams, sending Jacobson to third. The next hitter was Wally Gerber, who, while not known for his power, frequently came up with the clutch blow. Such was the case this time, though the weather was to be a factor. Gerber lofted a fly to Cardinal right fielder Jack Smith, who misjudged the ball and, once he started for it, was hampered by the soggy field. The ball dropped in, and Jacobson scored from third with the winning run.

Once again both pitchers had gone nine innings, and once again Shocker was the victor, giving up nine hits and striking out seven. The Browns' two earlier runs had come on a Hank Severeid home run with one on in the second, repeating Williams' similar blast the week before. Mid-season form again prevailed when Shocker pitched himself out of a jam in the eighth. With two out, Stock singled and Hornsby doubled. Mueller was intentionally walked to set up the force play. McHenry then solidly hit Shocker's first offering, but it went right to McManus, who threw him out at first. Earlier in the sixth Tobin had demonstrated his throwing arm when he threw out Stock at the plate as the latter attempted to score from second base. Again the weather aided the Browns as the muddy base paths slowed Stock and the ball arrived at Severeid some ten feet ahead of him.

The game had some other unique aspects. For one thing, it marked the first use ever of the Cardinal logo of two red birds on a bat and the word "Cardinals" across the front (the logo still in use today). Another notable event came in the ninth, while Jacobson was batting. The Browns protested that Sherdel had delivered a strike without taking his position on the rubber. The squad crowded around umpire Richard Nallin, and Jimmy Austin became so vocal that Fohl had to bodily remove him from Nallin's presence. The uproar proved to be inspirational as Jacobson got his single on the next pitch.

The weather cleared on Sunday, April 9, and an all-time St. Louis crowd of some 29,000 turned out for the final game of the spring series. As early as 10:30 a.m., spectators began to gather, and by 1:00 p.m., two hours before game time, all reserved seats were sold. As was common practice in those days, ropes were stretched in front of the outfield pavilions to accommodate the overflow. This crowd would see an unusual game in which eight runners, five Cardinals and three Browns, were thrown out at the plate.

As he had done in New Orleans the previous Sunday, Fohl sent Vangilder to the mound, this time as a starter, for his final tune-up before the season opener in Chicago the following Wednesday. The veteran righthander responded by going the distance, though he gave up a dozen hits. He was aided by some masterful outfield play on the part of Ken Williams. In the first inning Williams went back into the spectators to grab Mueller's fly ball and then pegged to Severeid to nail Bottomly at the plate. In the third Williams duplicated this effort by catching McHenry's fly and getting Stock at home. In the previous inning he nailed Ainsmith at second base as the Cardinal catcher attempted to stretch a single into a double.

Although the game was a relatively easy victory for the Browns as they went ahead in the fifth to ultimately win 6–3, it was not without its low points. George Sisler, who would lead the American League in stolen bases, was thrown out at home on three occasions trying to score on hits or infield outs. Jacobson, Saturday's hero, went hitless, striking out twice.

"Thank goodness, that's over," Stockton quoted Fohl after the game. Despite the efforts of both clubs to downplay the city series, it was evident by the closeness and intensity of the action in the four games that the inter-city competition mattered greatly to both fans and players alike. The Browns belied their own concern when it was later revealed that Phil Ball had awarded each Brownie $100 for retaining the city title.

The *Sporting News* commented facetiously after describing the four games: "The desperate character of the Sunday game is indicated by the fact that no less than eight runners were thrown out at home. Do the players and fans want these games? Not on your life, they just hate to think of playing or seeing them."

Thus spring training concluded on a highly optimistic note and a final 20-1 record. The latter broke down into 4-1 against major league opposition, 14-0 versus minor league teams, and 2-0 against the colleges.

2

APRIL

Kenny Williams Took a Bat and Gave a Baseball Three Long Whacks

Bob Quinn, in conjunction with Lee Fohl; had been busy during the spring in finding homes for those players who would not be retained on the roster. By the time the city series ended the squad was down to 26 players, with only reserve catcher Arthur Watkins remaining to be farmed out. Quinn performed a myriad of functions and held the title of vice president, but was also known as business manager and would today be called the general manager. Ray Gillespie recalled Quinn:

> Bob Quinn was one of the finest men I ever met. He served as a buffer between Phil Ball and the press and the outside world in general. He and he alone could handle Phil Ball during his cranky spells. Quinn was ready, willing, and able to talk to newspaper men at all hours of the night and day . . . and while passes were scarce in the limited seating at Sportsman's Park (18,000 capacity) in those days, Quinn was never stingy with the press, often giving writers a book of passes to be used whenever needed.

Quinn was born in Columbus, Ohio, on February 14, 1870. As a young man he had become a stonemason and played baseball on the side. Like his boss, Phil Ball, he was also a catcher in the minors. Giving up active playing because of an arm problem, Quinn became business manager of the Columbus American Association team in 1901. He held that position until the team was sold after the 1916 season. At that time his name came up as a possible buyer of the Cardinals, but the price proved to be too high. Ball hired him in April 1917 after deciding to let Branch Rickey move over to those same Cardinals, precluding what was expected to be a long legal hassle. Ball had at first sought legal means to prevent the Rickey action.

As the team headed for Chicago on April 10 there was a restrained optimism about their pennant chances. The restraint always centered around the pitching. Ray Gillespie shared the optimism:

> We recognized that the team was a natural winner and hoped that the meager pitching and excellent hitting and fielding would be enough to overtake the Yanks.... Urban Shocker was their best pitcher. "Dixie" Davis, Hubie Pruett, Dave Danforth, Elam Vangilder made up the rest of the staff with Ray Kolp, a converted shortstop, becoming a 14-4 pitcher. The Yanks had pitchers like Bob Shawkey, Joe Bush, Waite Hoyt, Carl Mays, to name a few. However, the Browns' hitters offset the Yank's pitching. Ken Williams, George Sisler (who had a fabulous year), Bill (Baby Doll) Jacobson, Hank Severeid were their sluggers; Johnny Tobin bunted around .300 with his swinging bunt and was the terror of the American League....

Stockton analyzed each Browns' pitcher:

> Schoker – Last year won 27 and lost 12. In fine condition this year and with the pennant possibility to spur him on he ought to lead the league and win 30 games.
>
> Bayne – Bill finished strong last year with a record of 11 and 5. This year he looks even better. His control is improved, his confidence increased and he may well be expected to be one of the best in the league. He ought to win twice as many games as last season.

The command group: Coaches Jimmy Austin (left) and Lefty Leifield (right) flank Manager Lee Fohl. (Photo courtesy of the *St. Louis Post-Dispatch*.)

Vangilder – Here is another pitcher for whom great things are predicted. Last season he won 10 and lost a dozen, which is a very poor performance, indeed, for a man of Vangilder's possibilities. He has hurled brilliantly this spring and like Bayne is expected to have the fine season which critics expected before this.

Davis – "Dixie" is considered a much better pitcher than his record of 15 and 16 of last season indicates. If he does not win 10 more than he loses it will be a big disappointment. His

> improved control over last year indicates a good year for him and the pennant talk of his comrades is expected to spur him on.
>
> Kolp–This youngster, with the confidence and cockiness of a veteran, won 8 and lost 7 last year. He has pitched some great games and can be expected to improve materially with the last season's experience behind him. This spring he has looked very good and at times very wild and ineffective.
>
> Danforth–Here is the big question mark of the Browns' staff. Obtained from Columbus in the 8 for 1 trade, his fate in American League circles cannot be predicted. His work in exhibition games, after his late arrival, has been encouraging. He is a clean, intelligent chap, always experimenting, always eager to learn more. He can be counted on to give the best he has.
>
> These men are considered the big six, the regular or first string pitchers. In addition there will be a number of youths who may produce a winner. Pruett, Meine, and Henry are considered the best prospects. . . .

Stockton then continued his evaluation of the Browns' chances by commenting on the positions:

> Sisler at first, can be counted on to perform brilliantly as last year, when he hit .371 and fielded .993.
>
> McManus, green and unreliable early last year, appears this year to be a potential star of the first class. There is every reason to be confident that he will bat much better than the .260 of last year and to be more reliable as a fielder. Last season his defensive average was .952. At second the Browns are much stronger than they were during the major part of last season.
>
> Gerber, who batted .278 and fielded .943 last year, and who is far more dangerous as a batter than his average indicates, also gives promise of having a year as good as he did in 1921. He is a fine shortstop, follows a ball perfectly and can hold his own with any in the league.
>
> Frank Ellerbe's work this spring has drawn much praise. He has manipulated plays of surpassing brilliance, but there are many among the Browns' close followers who will whisper when cornered that Ellerbe's 1922 performance will determine the Browns' success or failure. The belief

> appears to be that only at third is the strength of the Browns' inner line questionable. Fohl is ready to stand or fall on Ellerbe's work. He will bet on him. And after watching "Guv" in the spring games the writer is inclined to string with Fohl. Ellerbe has the fighting spirit, the winning spirit, and everybody who has seen him asserts that he is playing better than he ever did for Washington.
>
> Fohl's outfield of Tobin, Jacobson, and Williams is intact from last year, and barring accidents, should perform as well in the field and at bat as last season, when Tobin and Jake hit .352 and Williams .347.
>
> Behind the bat the Browns will be better fortified than they were last season. Collins has improved steadily and will do much of the catching. He is certain to hit far above his 1921 average of .243. Severeid this spring indicates that his bat which knocked the ball for .324 last season will do as well this campaign. Billings should improve over his work last year, though Collins and Severeid will do the bulk of the receiving.
>
> The better pitching staff and a far superior infield, therefore, are the engines which must haul the Browns up from third to first place, if that pinnacle is to be attained. And nobody knows better than St. Louisans what fragile things pitching staffs are. There's a mighty steep hill between April 12 and a pennant, with all the Browns' improvement.

The *Sporting News* made some observations on Lee Fohl and the American League race in general:

> Over in the camp of the Browns Manager Lee Fohl was all smiles and almost rivaled Jimmy Austin in the hustle and pep he showed. Lee is so confident of his team he's actually getting kittenish. And well he may, not many ball clubs in the American League are going to beat the kind of play the Browns put up Saturday and Sunday.... Yankees, of course are picked to win in the American, no guesser has been found to give any other club more than a fighting chance against them. Washington is a favorite second place team, with the Browns and Indians pretty even in the choice for third place. A current of opinion runs through the comments that the race in the American is going to be more of a scramble than in the National.

The consensus among baseball people and writers in the spring of 1922 was that the Yankees were likely repeaters. The only question that existed was what effect the absence of Babe Ruth and Bob Meusel would have during the first five weeks of the season. Both had been suspended after the prior season for participating in a post–World Series barnstorming tour. While such tours were common at the time, players for teams participating in the World Series were prohibited by baseball law from taking part. The Yankees had won their first American League pennant in 1921 and then lost the World Series to their Polo Grounds landlords, the Giants, five games to three. Both Ruth and Meusel as well as pitcher Bill Piercy (traded to Boston for 1922) were aware of the rule, but decided to defy Commissioner Landis. Landis quickly responded by suspending all three until May 20, 1922, though they were allowed to participate in spring training and in in-season exhibition games up to that date. As the fates would have it, the first game back for Ruth and Meusel would be against the Browns at the Polo Grounds.

The Browns opened the season at Comiskey Park against the White Sox on April 12. As expected, Fohl sent Urban Shocker out to initiate what was to be the club's most artistic season. Shocker allowed the Sox nine hits, but gave them up in the right places as St. Louis won 3–2. It was a heartbreaking loss for Chicago pitcher Urban Faber, who gave up only a double to Sisler and singles to Jacobson and Severeid, but walked three. Two of the walks came at the wrong time and developed into runs.

Fohl wasted little time in getting Dave Danforth into action against major league opposition the next day. Facing his former team, the southpaw pitched brilliantly until the eighth, when wildness caused him to walk four men, allowing a run to score.

***Opposite*: The pitchers. Kneeling, left to right: "Dixie" Davis, Urban Shocker, Bill Bayne, and Ray Kolp. Standing, left to right: Wayne Wright, Overlook, Dave Danforth, Frank Henry. Overlook was cut in spring training. Henry appeared briefly with the team, but spent most of the season with Mobile of the Southern Association. (Photo courtesy of the *St. Louis Post-Dispatch*.)**

The catchers. Kneeling, left to right: Hank Severeid, Arthur Watkins. Standing, left to right: Josh Billings, John Heving, and Pat Collins. Both Watkins and Heving were cut in spring training. (Photo courtesy of the *St. Louis Post-Dispatch.*)

He was saved by a great shoestring catch by "Baby Doll" Jacobson, who turned the catch into an inning-ending double play to preserve the 4–2 victory.

The umpires were suspicious of Danforth's motion to first base, as the Texas native later related to Stockton:

> He'd [umpire George Moriarity] heard so much about my balk motion and about my using a fresh ball that he thought

> he ought to say something. He looked at the ball and came out to the mound and told me I could not get away with anything and to be more sure he stepped straight toward first base when I threw there. But he found nothing to indicate I was "slicking" him.

As the season progressed Danforth was to be the continual target of umpires as they became concerned not so much with the "balk" move, but with a general feeling that Danforth was doctoring the ball. Danforth would consistently deny this, but the matter ultimately led to Fohl's disenchantment with him.

The third game of the series was rained out, and the rest seemed to do the Browns good as they pounded five White Sox pitchers for 21 hits and a 14–0 victory. Among the hits was a home run by Frank Ellerbe, his only one of the year. Vangilder limited Chicago to but three hits. Perhaps the Browns were basking in the light of a Lee Fohl treat; the night before the rain-out, he had taken some players out and cooked a meal while Jimmy Austin reportedly served as waiter and dishwasher. Or perhaps they were still in a jovial frame of mind from the circus they had seen the previous evening. Whatever the inspiration, it was the first example of the type of awesome attack the team was capable of, one that would be repeated on a number of occasions.

Moving on to Cleveland after the three-game sweep and a tie for first with the Yankees, the pennant express received a rude derailment. Cleveland was always a jinx opponent for St. Louis, and the opening series seemed to indicate the trend would continue in 1922. With a rain-out in between, the Indians won the first two games of the set, slamming Kolp, Bayne, and Henry for 22 hits in a 17–2 romp in the second game. It was to be the Browns' worst single defeat of the year. But they came back on April 19 to turn the tables on Cleveland 15–1. Vangilder again pitched a nine-inning three-hitter and added a home run to make the victory even sweeter. The Cape Girardeau, Missouri, native was an excellent hitter and Fohl later used him as a pinch-hitter. Speaking in the venacular of his birthplace, he would later reflect:

"I jus' thought a pitcher hadn't anything to do, but stand up there and take three strikes, but I reckoned I'd help myself along by swinging at a few and I'm getting so now I don't get sore at myself."

Both Sisler and Williams stole three bases each, and the club returned to St. Louis and the home opener on a high note. But the joy was to be short-lived as the White Sox sought revenge for their three losses in Chicago.

Some 12,000 fans were on hand at Sportsman's Park on April 20 when St. Louis Mayor Kiel opened the season by throwing the first ball to President Aloe of the Board of Aldermen. After three tries Aloe popped up to Frank Ellerbe. It was to be Ellerbe's best play of the day, as his first-inning muff of a pop-up permitted two runs to score, runs which proved to be the difference in the 4–2 defeat. Shocker went all the way for the loss, scattering eight hits. Phil Ball's good friend American League president Ban Johnson was on hand and shared Ball's private box along with vice president Walter Fritsch. As might be expected in the presence of a close friend, Johnson was effusive about the Browns' chances, according to the *Post-Dispatch*:

> I saw the Browns in their two spring series games with the Cardinals and I cannot see where the Yanks even with Ruth and Meusel in the line up, are one whit superior. St. Louis has a team with plenty of speed and lots of hitting strength with pitching its only questionable asset. While New York may have individual sluggers who surpass the Browns' hitters I must confess that I believe St. Louis to be the better of the two. At the present time New York surpasses St. Louis only in its pitching strength.

The questionable pitching proved to be the club's undoing the next day. Danforth took a 4–2 lead into the ninth, only to falter and allow Chicago to tie the game. The Sox then blasted relievers Bayne and Kolp for six runs in the tenth and a 10–5 victory.

If all was not joy in St. Louis on April 21, the very next day would mark the beginning of an era in the season that would

The infielders. Kneeling, left to right: George Sisler, Wally Gerber, Marty McManus, and Jimmy Austin. Standing, left to right: Gene Robertson, Frank Ellerbe, and Herman Bronkie. (Photo courtesy of the *St. Louis Post-Dispatch*.)

bring great joy, not only to all St. Louis, but in particular to left fielder Ken Williams. Prior to that date no American League player had hit more than two home runs in a game, a particularly surprising fact in view of Babe Ruth's performances in 1920 and 1921 when he hit 54 and 59 respectively. In the National League both Bobby Lowe of Boston and Ed Delehanty of Philadelphia had hit four in a game back in the century's first decade, during the heart of the dead ball era. Not only would Williams establish a new American League record, but he would procede to hit seven home runs in nine games.

With only a few more than 3,000 fans on hand, it all began innocently enough. In the Browns' first, with Sisler on first and one run in, Williams belted Jose Acosta's third offering beyond the bleacher wall and out onto Grand Avenue. He was retired the next time, but in the sixth Sisler led off with a single and Williams followed with his second home run, a line-drive type as opposed to the tape measure blast of the first inning. By the time Williams came to bat in the seventh the Browns were ahead 7–3 and two were out. Sisler singled and eventually advanced to third. "Lum" Davenport, who had relieved Acosta after number two, then served up the record breaker. With such a performance one might think that the game was an easy victory. "Dixie" Davis had taken a 10–3 lead into the ninth, but his old wildness bugaboo got to him, and before it was over four runs were in and Shocker had to put out the fire.

Kenneth Roy Williams was born and raised in Grant's Pass, Oregon. Turning professional in 1913, he played with Regina and Edmonton in the Western Canada League before his contract was purchased by the Cincinnati Reds. Williams then shuffled between Cincinnati and Spokane or Portland of the Pacific Coast League until the close of the 1917 season. His 26 home runs with Portland in that season caught the eye of Bob Quinn, who purchased him for 1918 delivery to the Browns. World War I service limited the converted third baseman to only two games in 1918, and while he hit .300 in 65 games the following year, it was not until 1920 that he established himself as a regular. His .307 and .347 averages in 1920 and 1921, respectively, earned him solid star status. The lefthanded hitter's 24 home runs in 1921 had tied him with the Yankees' Bob Meusel for second place in the American League next to Ruth.

Williams' achievement was naturally hailed in St. Louis, but the city's correspondent to the *Sporting News* lamented his status in relation to that of Ruth:

> A photographer was told to go out and get a picture of Ken Williams swinging at the plate—and the well meaning camera artist proceeded to shoot Bill Jacobson. . . . Imagine the text and illustration that would have been incident to Babe Ruth hitting three home runs in one ball game! Sporting editors would have wired every syndicate in operation to rush story and photographs. But Ken hits three of them and a photographer on the ground doesn't even know which is Ken or Bill Jacobson. . . .

The home runs and the victories continued:

April 23. Browns 4, Chicago 2. Number four off righthander Clarence Hodge, with the bases empty.

April 24. Browns 6, Detroit 2. Number five off lefthander "Red" Oldham, with one on.

April 25. Browns 5, Detroit 3. Number six off righthander Howard Emke, with one on.

April 28. Browns 3, Cleveland 2. Number seven off lefthander "Duster" Mails, with the bases empty.

April 29. Browns 6, Cleveland 5. Numbers eight and nine off righthander Stan Coveleski, the first with one on and the other with the bases empty.

The Browns lost only once during the Williams rampage, 2–0 to Detroit on April 26, and closed out the month with an 11–9 victory over Cleveland on April 30. Both games were noteworthy because of the absence of a Williams home run, and in the case of the Cleveland game, the Indians executed a triple play. While the home run streak was the big news, the pitching was superb. Vangilder and Shocker turned in two nine-inning efforts each to bring their respective records to 4-0 and 4-2 by April 30. On that date the team was tied for first place with the Yankees with an 11-5 record.

St. Louis showed its appreciation to Williams on April 30 before the Cleveland victory by presenting him with a phonograph. Mr. J. E. Shertz, an enthusiastic fan, raised the money for the project, while the president of the Board of Police Commissioners, Mr. Phil Brockman, made the presentation. In

The outfielders. Kneeling, left to right: "Chick" Shorten and Cedric Durst. Standing, left to right: "Baby Doll" Jacobson, Ken Williams, and Johnny Tobin. (Photo courtesy of the *St. Louis Post-Dispatch*.)

what must be the pun of all puns, the *Post-Dispatch* headlined on May 1: "Having given him a new phonograph, the fans expect Williams to break all the old records."

Williams received relatively little attention, perhaps a reflection of the overwhelming dominance of Babe Ruth on the American sports scene in the 1920s. Ruth was sitting out his suspension, and there was more concern with that fact in the press of the day than with anything else. Perhaps if Williams had played in New York he might have received more attention, but the contrasting personalities of the two men also played a role. Off the field Ruth could be summarized by three "b's": bucks, booze, and broads. Williams had nowhere near the flamboyancy of Ruth – indeed, it is doubtful that anyone in that era could have come close – and was simply the poor country boy who made good. The *Sporting News* provided a brief profile:

> Kenneth Williams, this new home run feature of the American League, is a funny sort of guy. He actually plays ball as if he liked the game. Yes sir, never golfs, signs up with the movies or anything like that – and he talks baseball night and day. He's as different from Babe Ruth that it's almost a crime.
>
> Now the Babe has a different suit for every hour of the day, special pants, golf sticks, and all that sort of thing. But Ken Williams – he just lives in a two room efficiency apartment, goes to bed at night when he isn't hanging around the corner with the boys talking baseball – he is so different.
>
> Fact is, Williams actually bores some people the way he rants about baseball on and off the field – umpires in particular. Which brings on a story. There was a dispute in one of the games of the series between the Browns and Tigers in St. Louis. Williams ran in clear from left field to take it up:
>
> "Go back to the outfield," said Umpire George Hildebrand. "Your team's got a catcher here and a manager to make an argument."
>
> "Yes, I know," answered Ken Williams, "but, gosh, Hildy, I'm so interested in my work I just got to get in here and fight." . . .
>
> He is quite modest about his homers this season. Just the breaks he says. It has so happened he's been up when he had a chance to swing – no inside stuff – and he swung.
>
> "But," says the conscientious Kenneth. "We'll have to play a lot of inside ball later, when I'll be called upon to bunt, and then no homers, but if it happens I'm free to swing just watch'em sail."

The *Post-Dispatch*'s L. C. Davis paid one of St. Louis's highest tributes to Williams by featuring him in one of his poems:

Whose name is now on every tongue? Ken Williams
Whose praises now are daily sung? Ken Williams
Who is the rooter's joy and pride?
Who gives the pesky pill a ride,
And separates it from its hide? Ken Williams

Who is our most admired youth? Ken Williams
Who makes the fans forget Babe Ruth? Ken Williams
Who is the guy so calm and cool?
Who swings his trusty batting tool?
And knocks the pellet for a gool? Ken Williams.

3

MAY

Welcome Back, Babe

May started on an optimistic note: The Browns took sole possession of first place with a 13–2 romp over Cleveland in the finale of a four-game sweep. Ray Kolp went the distance, while the Browns' sluggers pounded out sixteen hits to include three doubles, two triples, and a home run by McManus. The victory ended the brief home stand, and the club now embarked on a road trip that would see them spend most of the month away from Sportsman's Park.

Detroit was the first stop, and the club's good fortune came to a quick halt when the Tigers won the first two games. The second loss, after a rain-out, was particularly demoralizing as Vangilder had the game won going into the ninth, but Cobb's double, Veach's single, and Harry Heilman's home run produced a 6–5 loss. The final game of the series was salvaged on May 5 when Bill Bayne hurled a no-hitter for eight innings, only to lose it in the ninth. It was to be the closest any St. Louis pitcher would come to a no-hitter during this memorable season.

Bayne was a Pittsburgh native who was signed by the Browns and sent to Tulsa for the 1919 season. Winning eighteen games there, he was called up to the big team at the tail end of the season. Some 58 years later, in an interview with *St. Louis*

Globe Democrat executive sports editor Bob Burnes, he recalled beating the Yankees in New York in his debut and savoring one of the fruits of victory in the big city:

> My roommate, Elam Vangilder, and I went for a walk and we went down to Times Square. The *New York Times*, as you probably know, had a message board like a lighted ticker tape outside the building. They got around to the ball scores and I saw my name in lights for the first time—"winning pitcher, Bayne"—and I'll tell you, I've never had as much a thrill from anything as I did from that.

Bayne was so enthralled that he and Vangilder stood there and watched the report come up in lights five times. "Van told me finally that I could stay there all night if I wanted, but he was going back to the hotel," Bayne said, laughing, "so I went with him."

Bayne also recalled some advice that Lee Fohl gave him:

> When I came up, Lee Fohl was the manager. He was a good one. I'll never forget two things he told me right away. He wanted to see me pitch and I kept throwing curve balls. He finally insisted on seeing my fast ball. I showed him and Lee grinned and said, "Now I know why you showed me the curve—but you are going to have to use the fast ball sometimes so keep working on it." . . . The other was the best piece of advice anybody ever gave me. Fohl said, "Son, when you are out there on the mound, just remember there are only two people in the ball park—you and the catcher. Don't worry about anybody else," and I've never forgotten it.

Three years later lefthander Bayne would reach the pinnacle of his baseball career with his two-hitter against Detroit. The Browns had given him a solid 6–0 lead going into the Tiger ninth, but Manager Ty Cobb was facing the prospect of having two no-hitters thrown against his team within the span of a week. On April 30 Chicago White Sox pitcher Charley Robertson had pitched a perfect game against Cobb's team, and the "Georgia Peach" was not about to have a repetition occur. Cobb sent righthanded reserve catcher Larry Woodall to pinch-hit to lead off the bottom of the ninth, and Woodall lined a single to left, which Ken Williams nearly caught. Bobby Veach added another single to further break the spell, and one run eventually scored on Harry Heilmann's sacrifice fly. But Bayne's greatest satisfaction came when Cobb removed himself for a righthanded pinch-hitter. Bob "Fats" Fothergill was the only man to pinch-hit for Cobb once his career was established, and in this case he flied out.

Bayne recalled that Cobb

> was a tough competitor. You know how he was. When he'd get on base, he'd point toward second and say, "This is my territory, from here to there, and I don't want anybody getting in my way" and if anybody did, he'd cut them down.... Well, one day I struck him out with my good curve ball. Ty was upset and yelled at me that I couldn't do it again. The next time he came up he reminded me. I went to 3-1 on him, then got him on two more curves. He ran right out to the mound and I thought he was going to start a fight. But he slapped me on the pants, and said, "I didn't think you could do it, but you did," and kept right on running out to center field.

Frank Ellerbe also recalled Cobb:

> "...right up there, one of the best, greatest of all time. He could do it all. A good outfielder, a good hitter, a great base stealer, kept his spikes sharp, they knew to give him the base line."
>
> Did Cobb actually use a file to keep his spikes sharp?
>
> "I didn't walk any closer than fifty-sixty yards from him, but I went out to the ball park there in Detroit one day and I saw him sitting over there and it looked to me certainly that he had a file filing his spikes."

Ellerbe further recalls an incident between himself and Cobb:

> He was on first base and a ball was hit to right field and the baseball was thrown to me at third. And as Ty came in he had a way of sliding in and hitting the base and popping right up on his feet so he could go to another base if the ball went by anything. But the ball was over to the side a bit and I grabbed the ball and came in to cut him down as he slid into the base and he went to pop up on his feet when my right shoulder hit him, knocked him back on his can. He jumped up and kicked back between my legs. I said, "Ty, if you kicked me on the shin I would have busted you between the eyes with this ball if it was the last thing I ever did." Cobb: "Oh kid go on and play your third base, go on by God!"
>
> Next day I went out to the ball park and Ty was sittin over on the dugout on their side. Cobb said, "Hey, Gov, come by here." I went over. "I hear you're quite a bird hunter and keep bird dogs and all. I bird hunt a lot every winter. I got two dogs back here under the stands where I keep 'em." [Cobb showed Ellerbe his "kennel" under the grandstand. After seeing the animals the conversation turned to baseball] . . . Cobb said, "Hey, Gov, I understand you're using the same model bat I use." I said, "Yeah, Ty, that's the old Hy Davis model." He said, "Well I just got in a new order of two dozen brand new ones. I want to give you one of them." He went to the dressing room and got me a nice one of his model bats with his name on it and gave it to me. He meant to show me that he didn't mean anything (about the sliding incident.) He had to be high strung and fiery to be the ball player he was. Oh, if you played in on him, if you played him deep, or ordinary back, if they needed one run he'd just dump one right down the third base line and beat it out at first. He was left handed you know. If you played in too close on him he'd chuck one down your throat or by you.

The Browns moved on to Cleveland and split the two-game series there as Shocker lost his second game in a row in the opener. The wind played havoc with Ken Williams' home run total; two potential four-baggers were blown back in for harmless outs. Kolp went the distance on May 7 for the 10–7 victory as the Browns pounded four Cleveland pitchers for fourteen hits.

The year's first invasion of the East began on May 8 in Washington when Fohl sent Danforth to the hill for the first time in two weeks. The *Post-Dispatch* commented: "Today promised to be a real test for his alleged questionable methods. It was learned that Umpire Billy Evans had been instructed to suspend Danforth for 10 days if he found him to be 'doctoring' the ball."

While the Browns won the game in the ninth when Ken Williams' double-scored Jacobson and Severeid, Danforth had departed by the third inning, prompting L. C. Davis to observe: "Danforth may not have roughened the ball, but those Senators surely treated it rough."

Tobin's home run and Bayne's relief pitching won the second game 7–5, but "the Big Train," Walter Johnson, scattered nine hits to win for the Senators the next day 2–1. Fohl then gave Pruett his first career start, and while he was relieved in the fifth inning, Bayne and Shocker helped preserve his 5–3 victory.

Flush from a 3–1 series victory, St. Louis moved on to Philadelphia for a three-game set with Connie Mack's Athletics. Shocker regained his winning form with an eight-hit effort as the Browns brought out the long ball for an easy 13–4 win. Sisler, McManus, Shorten, and Williams all homered. Shorten replaced Jacobson in center field while the latter recovered from a hand injury. But the joy was to be short-lived as the Athletics won the next two games 7–4 and 13–3. Vangilder, Davis, and Pruett all proved to be ineffective on the mound. The *Sporting News* expressed its displeasure at these and earlier pitching lapses:

> It's most annoying to see twirlers do wonder stunts for three or four or five or six or seven innings, only to nullify it all by having one of those "bad" rounds. There is no excuse for a "bad inning" by a pitcher who is bearing down all the time and it is up to Fohl to teach his assortment of boxmen that going at full speed through the whole afternoon is the only way to get in the money.

As he would do so frequently during the season, Fohl went with his "money" pitcher in Urban Shocker to open a scheduled four-game set in Boston on May 16. And as he would do so frequently, Shocker won in eleven innings, 6–5. Williams' double, Severeid's single, an error, and Ellerbe's sacrifice fly produced the winning runs for St. Louis.

Things did not work out as well the following day as it was the Red Sox's turn to win a close one. This time it was at the expense of normally reliable second baseman Marty McManus. Until he had made an error in one of the Philadelphia games, McManus had handled 147 chances flawlessly. On May 17 he fell apart completely. Vangilder carried a 3–0 lead into the Boston ninth when McManus made successive errors on ground balls by Leibold and Menosky. Vangilder then walked former Brown Del Pratt to load the bases. Smith singled, scoring two runs, and Joe Dugan, who would later play a key role in the Yankees' pennant chase, filled the bases on a bunt single. Subsequent sacrifice flies by Burns and Eddie Foster, who like Dugan would play a corresponding role in the Browns' fight, brought in the tying and winning runs.

McManus was heartbroken, but Phil Ball showed his magnanimous side by wiring this telegram: "Forget it! This is another day. If we did not make mistakes we would all wear crowns—Ball."

McManus was buoyed by the message and the *Post-Dispatch* reported his reaction: "He's a real boss. Wait till we get to New York and I'll show him some real work out there on second."

Despite Ball's encouragement L. C. Davis could not resist the opportunity for this rhyme, entitled "The Critic":

He went to see McManus play
And saw him toss the game away
And so he thinks he'll play that way
Forever and forever.

McManus was a late developer and was working as a bookkeeper when World War I broke out. Drafted into the army, the

Chicago native wound up in Panama rather than France, and it was there that he began to play baseball with some degree of regularity. Signing with Tulsa of the Western League after the war, he went there and was eventually sold to the Browns at the close of 1920. He started as a reserve the following year and eventually won the second base job, hitting .260 with 64 RBI for the season. McManus got his chance when Joe Gedeon, the regular second baseman, was banished from baseball for his involvement in the Black Sox scandal.

McManus and the rest of the team had two days to ponder the first clash of the season with the Yankees in New York on Saturday, May 20, as rain washed out the final two games of the Red Sox series. The Yankee games were critical, not only because they were the first meetings of the season between the two leading pennant contenders, but because they marked the long-awaited return of Babe Ruth to the New York lineup.

L. C. Davis reflected on that particularly overriding aspect in one of his classic poems, entitled "Never Again":

Ken Williams' four base record grows apace
He's knocked eleven homers into space
Upon the Monarch's face there is a frown
Uneasy lies the head that wears a crown

The King of Swat is sitting in a box
And makes note of Kenny's four ply knocks
"Barnstorming stunts may be all right," said he
"But they are not what they're cracked up to be

"I thought I was bigger than the game
And that the Judge would tremble at my name
But now I have the wide world informed
No barns by me in future will be stormed

The reinstatement of Ruth and Meusel on May 20 had long been anticipated by the baseball public at large and the New York public in particular. The first reserved seat application had been received as far back as April 15. Box seats had been sold out well prior to game day, but the Yankee box office indicated that all other classes of tickets would be available that day. The New York City Police Department was alerted and prepared to handle the expected overflow crowd.

New York had played well in the absence of Ruth and Meusel and held a two-game lead over the Browns going into the opening game. But the Yankees were not the same without the most towering sports figure of the twenties – and perhaps all time – in the lineup. Both players were required to make formal application to Judge Landis for reinstatement, which was quickly granted on the morning of the 20th. Umpires Chill and Owens were so advised.

Ruth was honored in pre-game ceremonies with a number of presentations: a floral wreath from the National Vaudeville Association commemorating his off-season venture into show business, a silver bat, and a loving cup containing soil from the baseball diamond at St. Mary's School in Baltimore where the Babe played his first baseball. Applause greeted him earlier in the day when he first stepped on the field and took batting practice. Later the ovation grew in intensity as he chased flies in left field. It was to be perhaps the best response he would get for some time.

Outside the Polo Grounds the New York police greeted the day's first arrivals at 10 a.m. By noon some eighty police were in the area as the crowd surged into the park. They flowed in, steadily filling the stands to more than capacity and forcing some to sit in the aisles. There was a great rush between 1:30 and 2:00, after which things quieted down. The fans received some added entertainment from a stunt plane performing several thousand feet above the park.

Fohl, of course, started Shocker, and the old master gave the Yankees but three hits. Unfortunately one of these was a home run to Aaron Ward in the fifth inning with Frank Baker on board, which gave the Yankees a 2–0 lead. New York manager Miller Huggins started "Sad Sam" Jones, who stifled the Browns until the eighth inning. Tobin got on via one of his patented swinging bunts. After Gerber's ground-out got him to second, Williams' single scored the St. Louis right fielder with the Browns' first run.

The top of the ninth started innocently enough. Jones got both Severeid and Ellerbe to ground out to Ward, who stood to be the hero of the day. But fate was to take a different turn. Fohl sent Shorten up to hit for McManus, and he singled to center. Pat Collins batted for Shocker and singled off Yankee shortstop Everett Scott's glove as Shorten raced to third. This brought lead-off man Tobin to the plate. He sent an apparently harmless grounder to Wally Pipp at first base. Pipp bobbled the ball momentarily, but recovered in time to toss to Jones covering. The put-out seemed assured as umpire Ollie Chill gave the out sign, but Jones dropped the ball and Shorten scored the tying run! Jones, now thoroughly unnerved, then gave up a single to right to Gerber, scoring Collins from second with the go-ahead run and sending Tobin to third. Sisler was intentionally walked to load the bases, and then Ken Williams was unintentionally walked, forcing Tobin in from third with the Browns' fourth run. Bill Jacobson (playing his first game since his hand injury) then became the ninth Brown to come to bat in the inning and settled the matter without further doubt by hitting a grand slam home run into the left field seats. Seven runs had scored after the alleged third out had been recorded! Severeid then doubled, but Jones finally got it back by striking out Ellerbe.

Fohl brought in Bill Bayne to pitch the bottom of the ninth, and he retired the Yankees in order. The first batter he faced was Ruth, who grounded out to Sisler. The game was not only a humiliating defeat for the defending American League champions, but an inauspicious debut for the day's premier performer. In three prior plate appearances Shocker had struck out Ruth in the fourth inning on a two-and-one count, got him to pop up to McManus in the fourth, and in the sixth with one out retired him on a high hopper to Sisler. Meusel fared no better, matching the zero-for-four performance with one of his own.

Accounts of this remarkable game have appeared in a number

of books, principally biographies of Ruth. In describing what happened in the Polo Grounds after the alleged third out was made, Ruth's description as told to biographer Bob Considine is similar to that found in Frederick Lieb's previously cited work, Tom Meany's *The Yankee Story*, Marshall Smelser's *The Life That Ruth Built: A Biography*, and Robert Smith's *Babe Ruth's America*:

> From then on there was the craziest mix-up I ever saw. Some of our players were already in the showers and thought it was a gag when they were told to return to the field. "Hey, I saw Chill call that man out," I squawked, and I had plenty of company.
>
> In the meantime the fans were milling around on the ball field, and it took the special cops about 20 minutes to clear the field.
>
> It still makes me froth to think about what happened after that. Jones had cooled off and had lost his stuff by the time he returned to the rubber. There were a couple of blooper hits and bases on ball which tied the score, and then that big Jacobson came up with the bases filled and knocked a ball into the lower right field stands.
>
> The Browns scored seven runs after their last man had been called out, and beat us 8–2!
>
> If ever there was a wild ball club it was in the clubhouse that night....

Interestingly enough neither Robert Creamer's *Babe: The Legend Comes to Life* nor Ken Sobol's *Babe Ruth and the American Dream* makes any mention of this less-than-common incident. More significantly, the newspapers of the day with the most reason to report the game in the greatest detail – the *New York Times, New York Daily News, St. Louis Post-Dispatch*, and the *Sporting News* – make no reference to crowds on the field or any game delay. Only an Associated Press wire story makes a brief reference to players starting to leave the field.

Frank Ellerbe, who made two of the Browns' three outs in the big ninth-inning rally, remembers it this way:

> It was the ninth inning with two men down. "Sad Sam" Jones was pitching, Wally Pipp was playing first base. Our

> lead-off man was Johnny Tobin, came to bat. He was a left-hand hitter, fast, a good drag man. He drug one down the first base line, Pipp runs in, fields the ball and pitches [underhanded] to Jones, the pitcher . . . at first base. . . . Just as the ball hits Jones' glove, he didn't hold it long enough, the umpire had already raised it [his hand], but then he had to call him safe. There was no big dispute about it a-tall. I think he dropped the ball without getting possession of it long enough. He [umpire] started to call him out I remember, but then he had to call him safe. But there was no argument from the fans or the manager. Miller Huggins was [the Yankees'] manager at the time and he didn't kick about it. There wasn't any kick about it, about the play, Ruth said there was, there wasn't much controversy.

Ellerbe said he did not recall the Yankees leaving the field, though he acknowledged that

> maybe they run right under (the stands) going to get the showers and all. And they might have been, Ruth and some of them, might have been halfway under there and leaving. But no crowd from the stands come on the field.

Another crowd of 40,000 was on hand for Sunday's game when the gates were thrown open at 11:30 a.m. Huggins started former Red Sox righthander Waite Hoyt, while Fohl countered with "Dixie" Davis. The Browns struck early, picking up two runs in the first inning when Tobin led off with a single and ultimately scored on Sisler's base hit. Sisler got the second run after stealing two consecutive bases when Yankee catcher Wally Schang's throw, attempting to nail Jacobson stealing, went into center field. New York pecked away at Davis, picking up four single runs over the first six innings. The fourth run involved Ruth's first hit of the season, a double that advanced Whitey Witt to third, whence he scored on Frank Baker's sacrifice fly.

St. Louis tied the game in the sixth when Gerber reached first on Baker's throwing error from third base. After the next two put-outs, one of which advanced Gerber to second, Jacobson singled him in and eventually scored after Severeid and Ellerbe's singles. The team traded runs in the seventh as Bayne made his second consecutive relief appearance. The game went into extra innings at 5–5. But there would be no repetition of Saturday's heroics. The Browns went down in their half of the tenth while Aaron Ward opened the New York half with a single to center. Jacobson bobbled the ball and Ward took second on the error. Ruth then came to bat with a chance to play the hero role, but the best he could do was advance Ward to third on his ground-out to McManus. But it was enough to set up the eventual winning run. Huggins went to his bench and sent reserve catcher Al Devormer up to hit for Frank Baker. Devormer responded by sending a grounder to Gerber as Ward dashed for the plate to score the winning run ahead of the throw.

It was more of the same on Monday as once again the Yankees went to extra innings for the victory. The difference this time was that the delinquent barn-stormers played a major role in the outcome. Fohl had started Vangilder, who had held New York scoreless until the last of the eighth as St. Louis led 3–0. Ruth had been unspectacular since his return. In this game he had popped out to Sisler, flied to Tobin, and walked. The initial good nature of the crowd since Saturday, excited by the return of the "messiah," had turned surly. In the seventh they cheered derisively as the Babe caught a simple fly. Ruth doffed his cap in simulated courtesy. The incident was repeated in the eighth. But all was forgiven when he slammed one of Vangilder's deliveries against the wooden facing between the upper tier and the roof to narrow the gap to 3–1. While the crowd may have been mollified, Ruth refused to tip his cap as he strode to the bench.

Vangilder ran into further trouble in the Yankee tenth. After retiring Pipp, Scott singled to center and Schang did the same to right. Tobin made an extremely bad throw to Ellerbe at third; it went to the stands, permitting Scott to score and Schang to go to second. Huggins then sent Camp Skinner up to hit for starting pitcher Bob Shawkey, and the young rookie promptly singled between Gerber and Ellerbe to score Schang with the tying run. (It was probably the most significant event of Skinner's brief major league career, which consisted of 34 games and a .196 batting average.) Fohl then went to the bull pen, choosing "Hub" Pruett to make the first of his many 1922 appearances against New York. Pruett retired the side and in the tenth began his magic against Ruth with a strike-out. By the time the 1922 season came to a close Pruett would establish himself as the most effective pitcher the Babe would ever face.

"Bullet Joe" Bush, who would pitch for the Browns in 1925, handled his future teammates with ease as he came on in relief of Shawkey. In the Yankee thirteenth, Meusel, who had been as frustrated as Ruth since his return, led off with a single to left. Pipp then sacrificed him to second, and Everett Scott became the hero with a base hit to right center. Meusel scored from second with the winning run. Pruett was the losing pitcher, but the *New York Times* made this observation: "Southpaw Pruett is just a youth–and a nice looking one, too. Now he can write and tell the folks that he struck out Ruth." Little did they know what lay ahead.

Although Shocker had worked eight innings on Saturday, he was back at it again as the Tuesday starter in the series finale. It was such use that would see the St. Louis ace log 348 innings pitched over the season, second in the league, despite being idled by an injury for over three weeks in June and early July. The Yankee hurler was the controversial Carl Mays. Mays had beaned Cleveland shortstop Roy Chapman during the 1920 season, and Chapman eventually died from the blow. Ray Gillespie recalled that all opposing clubs were "on" him as a result, and the Browns were no exception.

While a Browns victory would only restore the pennant race to where it was on Saturday morning, it was still critical in establishing the team as genuine pennant contenders. By the Browns' seventh the score was tied at 3–3, with the highlights to that point being home runs by George Sisler and Yankees' aging third baseman, Frank "Home Run" Baker. Mays led off the seventh by walking Shocker. After Tobin popped to Ward, Gerber singled to right, sending Shocker to second. Sisler then flied out to Ruth, but

Williams settled things for the day by hitting number 12 into the right field bleachers. Mays retired the side, but Huggins replaced him with Lefty O'Doul for the eighth and ninth innings. O'Doul would later distinguish himself as a hitter, winning the National League batting title in 1929, after being converted to an outfielder. The reason for the switch becomes apparent when one observes the Browns picking up five runs on four hits and four walks in this particular game. The final score was 11–3 as both Ruth and Meusel went hitless. The St. Louis club had given warning that it was to be taken seriously.

Joseph Holland, who was now covering the Browns for the *Post-Dispatch*, saw much reason to be encouraged by the series:

> New York's pitching is as good today as it will be at any time this season. The Yankee moundsmen showed excellent form in all four games and the inevitable conclusion is that the Brown attack is more than enough to cope with Hug's high priced and very tempermental hurling corps.... Hoyt and Mays have a host of enemies on their own club and that will count against them.
>
> New York played a straight away hitting game, one which is consistent with players of the Meusel-Ruth type. On the other hand the Browns mixed up their plays and showed a diversity of attack that kept the Yanks guessing all the time....
>
> The Browns made 17 more hits in 41 innings and scored 12 more runs. They pounded out 49 hits against 32 and scored 27 runs against 15. Still the Yanks gained a split in the series, but needed several breaks to put it over....
>
> The series has shown convincingly that the Yanks are not in with the pennant by any means. If the remainder of the Brown pitching staff helps Shocker out New York will have its pitching advantage offset by the inferior play of its team....

L. C. Davis added his bit of glee at the Browns' performance in New York by taking this jab at Ruth: "'Oh, he'll quit,' Babe Ruth is quoted as saying in discussing Ken Williams. 'He's only good on the St. Louis field.' Whereupon Ken proceeded to bang one into the bleachers with two on."

So while they still trailed the Yankees by two games, the Browns left New York on a high note–but their joy was to be short-lived. After a two-day trip west the club opened a four-game series against the White Sox on Friday, May 26. Chicago starter Ferdinand Schupp locked up with Bill Bayne in a pitcher's duel and settled the issue himself by knocking in the winning run with a single in the seventh. For the Saturday doubleheader Fohl went with Shocker in the first game and Vangilder in the night-cap. He was to be rewarded with two outstanding pitching efforts, but also two defeats as timely hitting and Wally Gerber's fielding left much to be desired.

Shocker had a perfect game, the pitcher's dream going into the eighth inning with a 1–0 lead. With one out Chicago left fielder "Bib" Falk broke the spell with a single. Ray Schalk, later a Hall of Famer, then doubled him in to tie the game. The Browns threatened in the top of the tenth, getting runners to first and third, but with no result. In the White Sox's half Eddie Collins, another Hall of Famer, turned an easy grounder to short into a two-base error as Gerber threw wild to Sisler. John Mostil sacrificed Collins to third and Falk came through again with a single to right, scoring the winning run. Shocker had given up but three hits while his teammates got eight off the "other Urban," Chicago ace Faber. He had come close to duplicating Charley Robertson's perfect game effort for these same White Sox when that otherwise undistinguished (lifetime record 49-80) hurler had performed the feat against Detroit 2–0 on April 30. But there was more bad news to come before the day was out.

Vangilder gave Chicago only six hits in the second game, which was good enough for a 2–0 lead until the Browns' eighth. The normally potent St. Louis bats had been strangely silent since the New York series, but came alive briefly. After Sisler flied out to open the inning Jacobson singled to right. Severeid flied out, but Williams was hit by a pitched ball. Frank Ellerbe then doubled off Chicago pitcher Henry Courtney, bringing home both Jacobson and Williams to tie the game. But once again Gerber was to be the goat. Mostil led off the Chicago ninth with an easy roller to Gerber only to have that otherwise reliable fielder duplicate his first game wild throw to Sisler. Mostil wound up at second and Falk's attempted sacrifice became a bunt single, sending Mostil to third. Schalk then squeezed Mostil home with a bunt to Ellerbe. "Gov" threw to Severeid at the plate, but umpire Wilson ruled Mostil safe with the winning run. That, as the *Post-Dispatch*'s Joe Holland put it, "shunted the Browns a long way behind the Yanks." Severeid was enraged by the call and threw the ball at Wilson, but the umpire took no action.

As the sun set over Chicago that evening the Browns could only console themselves with George Sisler's league-leading figures in hitting (.429), runs scored (39), hits (65), total bases (96), and stolen bases (18). To add further misery it was announced that player-coach Jimmy Austin had been fined $10 and suspended for three games for arguing a called third strike with umpire "Brick" Owens in Friday's game. Austin had pinch-hit for Bill Bayne.

Gerber's performance in the field during this doubleheader was far from typical. A native of Columbus, Ohio, the 5′ 10″ shortstop was regarded by many as the best at the position in the American League. The following year he handled 48 chances without an error, which stood as a major league record for some time. Gerber carried the nicknames "Maxie" and "Spooks," but was most commonly known as "Wally." He began his baseball career in the Ohio State League at Marion in 1910 and later played for Akron and Columbus before reaching the majors with Pittsburgh in 1914. Failing to dislodge the aging great, Honus Wagner, Gerber returned to his hometown Columbus team. By 1918 he was in St. Louis as the regular Browns shortstop, a position he would fill until early 1928.

Ray Gillespie remembers Gerber, along with Frank Ellerbe, as "just nice people":

> ...being a newspaper man why I like people to be nice to me and cooperative, and they were very friendly and gentlemen all the way. And when you asked them a question they gave you an answer which was different in the case of

Elam Russell Vangilder not only posted a 19-13 record, but hit .343 with two home runs in 1922. (Photo courtesy of Kenneth Vangilder.)

> a lot of the others. They were just high class people, good people to deal with, nice persons for a sportswriter to know.

Gerber batted .256 over his major league career, but in a number of key years with the Browns his average was more in the .270-.280 range. Though usually hitting in the eighth position in the order, he frequently came through with clutch hits. One of the most memorable of these would occur in 1925 when it proved to be the difference in the Browns finishing third over Detroit and thereby earning part of the World Series pot. The hit became known as the "$18,000 hit" after the amount divided up by the third-place finishers. At that time there was no money for finishing fourth.

The Browns salvaged the near disastrous series with Chicago by taking the Sunday game 4–2. Gerber redeemed himself to some extent by making a key play in the seventh which retired the side and cut off two potential runs. At bat he collected four singles in five trips as the Browns got six other singles and six walks off "Perfect Game" Charley Robertson.

Fohl's crew returned to Sportsman's Park on May 29 to begin their first extensive home stand of the season. At this point in time the club had played but ten games at home, and based on the *Sporting News* greeting on May 29, they were not exactly welcomed back with open arms:

> Mound City fans welcome their returning Browns with about the same feeling that a mother greets a young offspring who comes in from an afternoon's play all wet, muddy and bedraggled, with his shins barked and a bump over one eye. The fans want to know how come the Browns got that way and they're not in humor to accept alibis. A home coming with nothing better than an even break against anything except the Washingtons, who were caught in a slump, and for the windup of a road trip a bunch of lickings at the hands of the White Sox, doesn't bring out any welcoming bands....
>
> The fans are demanding that the Browns get a little sand

> and iron in their systems, take a leaf out of Urban Shocker's life and play the sort of never say die ball that hard boiled bird does, and if they don't they might as well stop counting World Series money—Shocker can't do it all; everybody from the manager down has to help....
>
> Manager Lee Fohl has one pitcher who will pitch, in Urban Shocker; two who can if they will, in Vangilder and Bayne, and one who may if given a chance in Pruett. That's four, not so many, but enough with a ball club behind them that's the best in the league on offense and defense. Of course Fohl has several other alleged pitchers—most of whom might as well be traded off for one good minor leaguer who has the courage to say he can and will. They need a pitcher like that one who is willing to take a chance; they sure do need something or somebody who believes in taking a chance and can make up his mind to take it. Safety first may do on the boulevards, but it never gets you anywhere on the speedway.

Whether stung by this rebuke or others, the Browns rebounded from the Chicago series and took the first of a four-game set with Detroit 9–6. Fohl started Davis, who faltered with a 9–2 lead after 6⅓ innings. Fortunately the lead held up, but not before the Tigers came up with four more runs off the combined efforts of Davis, Pruett, Kolp, and Vangilder. Williams' grand slam homer in the third inning, his thirteenth, had provided the Browns with early momentum.

Tuesday, May 30, was Memorial Day and the traditional morning-afternoon doubleheader was played before a big crowd. The *Post-Dispatch*'s J. Roy Stockton described the scene for the afternoon game:

> The reserved seats were sold early and the upper deck of the grandstand and pavilions were filled long before game time. When play started, spectators were lined in front of each pavilion. The attendance was estimated at 22,000. The bleachers, because of the heat, were not filled.

The morning game began at 10:00 a.m. Detroit played without Harry Heilman and Ty Cobb, who had been suspended as a result of an altercation with the umpires in the series opener. The absence didn't seem to hurt as Detroit won 6–5, defeating Bayne. The little-used Frank Henry relieved Bayne and was shelled for five hits and three runs in only two innings.

Afternoon games usually began at 3:00 p.m. and Memorial Day was no exception – though this particular game was exceptional in that it was the longest the Browns were to play in 1922. Fohl started Shocker, and the veteran righthander went 14⅓ innings, giving up eleven hits, but only one run. It was not the Tigers who put Shocker out of the game, but his and Tobin's vigorous protest over umpire Owens' ball and strike calls. Tobin was not only thrown out of the game, but suspended. But it mattered not as the reserves came to the rescue. With the game at 1–1 in the sixteenth, Cedric Durst, who took Tobin's place in right field, singled. After being sacrificed to second, Pat Collins, who had relieved Severeid behind the plate, singled Durst home with the winning run. "Hub" Pruett had set the stage for these heroics with some of his own. Relieving Shocker with one on and one out, the University of Missouri graduate struck out four of the remaining five batters that faced him and got the fifth to roll out to Ellerbe. The *Post-Dispatch* hailed him as "the college boy who saved the day."

Fohl once again went to Pruett as his bullpen ace the following day in the final game of the Detroit series. Carrying a 7–3 lead into the ninth, Vangilder became ineffective. L. C. Davis best describes the ending:

> Vangilder exploded, the bases were loaded
> When Pruett jumped into the breach
> Two heart rending errors for him had no terrors
> And he halted the tribe of the Peach (7–5 win)

While May closed optimistically with four victories in the last five games, the club slipped from a first-place tie with the Yankees on April 30 to a three-game deficit behind the league leaders.

4

JUNE

Troubles with Mays and Haney

As June began the Browns continued their winning ways by taking three of four games with Chicago, avenging the debacle of late May. "Dixie" Davis started the first game and went the distance, which in this case was 12 innings, giving up only four walks and seven hits in the 4–3 victory. As Frank Ellerbe would recall: "We used to say anytime 'Dixie' didn't walk over three or four batters he was a pretty sure winner." Davis was no stranger to extra-inning baseball. On August 9, 1921, the North Carolina native pitched 19 innings against the Washington Senators with the Browns winning 8–6 with two runs in the top of the nineteenth. Davis gave up only five walks over the course of the game, while George Sisler collected six hits in eight at-bats. Sisler also figured prominently in the game at hand as his single scored "Chick" Shorten from third with the winning run. Shorten was filling in for Johnny Tobin, who was still under suspension for the incident in the second game of the Memorial Day doubleheader.

On June 2 the club got another route-going effort as Shocker scattered fourteen hits while getting the same number from his teammates. Williams led the assault in the 12–4 victory by hitting home run number 14 in the third inning when the Browns batted around and scored seven runs. The White Sox came back the following day to win 5–4 in the ninth when pitcher Henry Courtney singled in the winning run much like his fellow moundsman Ferd Schupp had done the previous month. Fohl was encouraged by Danforth's middle-inning relief of Bayne when he held his old club hitless. The *Sporting News* commented: "Danforth twirled the major part of four innings and the White Sox were helpless before him. He went out to let Pat Collins hit a homer as a pinch hitter and tie the score – but of course Vangilder couldn't get his hoodoo ninth inning as a relief pitcher and the game was lost. . . ."

The series finale was another extra inning victory as Fohl went to Pruett, but used Shocker with only one day's rest in relief. Workhorse that he was, the Cleveland native responded with three strong innings, allowing one hit. Gerber's tenth inning single won the game 3–2. The *Sporting News* was now happier with the Browns' pitching staff and commented:

> Pruett showed he can pitch as a regular member in good standing of Shocker's pitching staff. Since all Shocker needs is a couple of guys with entrails to help him out now and then, the demonstration that Pruett and Danforth are a pair of that sort is important enough. It looks a bit more like pennant for the Browns than it did.

The Red Sox came to Sportsman's Park on June 6 and the overworked Shocker was once again called upon. Pitching with only a day's rest and with Tobin back in right field after his suspension, he gave Boston only six hits in the 5–2 win. Bill Jacobson homered in the first with one on. Things turned sour the next day as the Red Sox raked "Dixie" Davis for ten hits and a 7–3 triumph despite Marty McManus's home run. Vangilder's previously noted ineffectiveness continued on June 8 when he surrendered a grand slam home run to right fielder Elmer Smith as Boston built up a 7–1 lead over the first four innings. The Browns battled back, including Tobin's home run, but fell short 7–5. Fohl went to Danforth for the last game, and he responded with another strong effort in the 8–1 victory. While allowing only six hits, "Dauntless Dave" continued to have trouble with his move to first base, being called for two balks.

Trailing New York by two and one-half games, St. Louis now made ready for the first invasion of the hated Yankees. *Post-Dispatch* writer John Wray noted:

> After one four game series this spring at New York the Browns took away $37,000 net cash or more money than Robert Lee Hedges had invested in the team when these same Browns were brought into existence in 1902. The Yanks are due in St. Louis for a series. As early Tuesday every reserved seat for Saturday and Sunday had been sold out according to report.

L. C. Davis could not avoid his own observation: "The 'house' for the Browns-Yankee game on Saturday and Sunday was sold out a week in advance. Demonstrating that Babe Ruth can draw something besides suspensions."

Vangilder's problems, as well as those of the remainder of the pitching staff and the other players, always drew the quick ire of the St. Louis press. The *Sporting News* columnist John Sheridan was particularly critical of Vangilder:

> I saw a rare demonstration of just how not to pitch given by Elam Vangilder of the St. Louis Americans against the Boston Red Sox on June 8. Vangilder did everything that a pitcher should not do as long as he was in that game. In so much as Vangilder earned some reputation as a pitcher during April and May, it is almost unbelievable that he should pitch such ball as he pitched against the Red Sox on June 8, 1922. . . .
>
> No doubt that Vangilder lacked his "stuff" that day. He was hit hard from the start. But must a pitcher depend wholly upon "stuff." My idea of a pitcher is a man who can pitch good ball when his "stuff" is not with him, when his fast ball won't shoot or his curve ball break, when his control is none too good, etc. Anyone can throw "stuff" past batters. Using it is not really pitching ball. The real pitcher uses his head. His arm may be sore as a boil, his speed may be absent, his curve may not be acting right, they may be hitting

> him hard, but, by sheer device and gameness he pulls through and wins. That's a real pitcher as I judge them.

The regular correspondent of The *Sporting News* added his own acid-dripped comments:

> That one man pitching staff of the Browns has cracked under the strain and unless some of those other alleged to be pitchers show enough to step into the breach and earn some of the money they are drawing from Phil Ball, then Mr. Fan might as well be told and be done with it, not to figure on how he's going to get reservations for World Series games at Sportsman's Park....
>
> And the pitching staff isn't all of it. Look at the batting averages of the Browns: who's carrying the load there? George Sisler mostly, with some help by Tobin and Severeid. A .282 batting average for our late home run hero, Ken Williams; Jacobson and Ellerbe batting under .250. That batting order of Fohl's has to be harmonized if the Browns are going to live up to expectations.

There could be nobody but Urban Shocker to open a crucial series against the league leaders, but it was apparent that the great righthander was tired. With some 22,000 fans filling "the great ball yard from the grandstand aisles to the distant bleacher wall" as the *Sporting News*' J. Roy Stockton put it, events began positively enough. The Browns took an early 2–0 lead in their half of the first when Tobin drew a walk from Yankee starter Carl Mays and Gerber sacrificed him to second. After Sisler fouled out, Williams and Jacobson stroked successive singles to produce the only Browns lead of the game. The Yankees tied the score in the second—and all hell broke loose in the third.

Ruth homered with one on to break the tie, and an obviously unnerved Shocker hit Frank Baker, the Yankees' aging third baseman, in the right side of the back. Baker was later removed from the game and X-rayed at a St. Louis hospital. Physicians feared that a rib had been fractured, but this proved negative and Baker spent Saturday night at the team's hotel.

Meusel then doubled and Baker scored when Jacobson let the ball get away from him in attempting to throw. Meusel took third and Pipp singled him home. There then followed two errors on one play that further tried the weary Shocker. Scott hit an easy roller to Gerber, who threw to second, attempting to force Pipp and go for the double play. McManus recovered the ball and then he too threw wild to Ellerbe at third! Pipp easily scored while all this was going on, and Scott wound up on third. Catcher Al Devormer's fly ball scored Scott and brought Carl Mays to the plate.

What happened next is best described by the *Post-Dispatch*'s J. Roy Stockton:

> . . . when Carl Mays, the much hated pitching rival, came to the plate with a smile of ridicule on his face and a taunt on his lips, Shocker lost either his temper or his control.
>
> The first pitch to Mays was high and inside. So high and so far inside that had Mays not stepped quickly to one side the ball would have hit him in the head. No attention was paid to that. But the second pitch was almost a duplicate and this time Mays arose, dusted off his uniform and said something to Shocker. Shocker stood on the mound nodding his head. He was saying "Yes" to whatever Mays was asking.
>
> Shocker would up slowly for his third pitch. The popular guess was that it was to be a slow ball. That windup, intended to give the impression that a fast one is coming, frequently is exaggerated by a pitcher when he means to send up a floater. But the guess was wrong. Again the ball sailed toward the batter, high and inside, and as it reached the batter's box it curved in and down and barely missed the jaw of the Yankee batter.
>
> Mays figured one ball near his head might be an accident and that the second might be a coincidence, but, by George, when a third one sailed at his head it looked too much like a habit and so he strode to the pitcher's box, clutching his bat in his hands behind him. Shocker heatedly answered whatever Mays said and the men stepped closer. It appeared that a fight was near and perhaps the quick action of Umpire Billy Evans did prevent a fistic encounter. Evans

> stepped between the men, gave each a shove and by that time the slow walking police had reached the scene. Both would be belligerents were surrounded and led to their proper places and the game went on.

Shocker then walked Mays and faced Whitey Witt, the New York lead-off man who would later in the season play a key role in the final September series between the two rivals. Shocker was not through with the close pitches. Again Stockton recounts:

> Witt, the next Yankee batter, had to tumble in the dust to avoid being hit by Shocker's first pitch to him, and the Yankee, scrambling to his feet, rushed belligerently to the mound and again the umpires and police had to step double quick to prevent an exchange of blows.
>
> By this time the mob was howling in great volume. Some wanted Mays' life immediately, and some were booing Shocker and most of them were just yelling on general principles, because, the game being hopelessly lost, there was nothing in particular to yell about.

Shocker eventually retired the side, but six runs had come across the plate for an 8–2 Yankee lead and Fohl realized the game was impossible to retrieve. Bayne and Wright gave up another six runs between them before Pruett finished up strongly. Robertson replaced Gerber at short in the fifth inning; Durst and Shorten successively relieved Tobin in right field; and Collins went behind the plate as Fohl sought to rest some regulars and give selected reserves some playing time. One of these reserves, Gene Robertson, would add the final indignity of the day to the Browns' efforts. Batting in the seventh, Robertson lofted a pop fly foul just behind the Browns' dugout. The ball struck none other than owner Phil Ball, who was conversing with team vice president Walter Frisch. The blow required four stiches in Ball's left cheek from team physician Dr. Robert Hyland. While there was no fracture, the St. Louis owner suffered a slight brain concussion and severe shock. After treatment at St. John's Hospital the volatile Ball insisted on being taken to his home. The final

New York victory margin was 14–5, thus bringing to a close one of the darker days of this 1922 Browns season.

Sunday's game brought out another large crowd, this time estimated at about 25,000. The numbers were so great that they overflowed onto the playing field and made ground rules necessary. Sunday's game also brought Urban Shocker back for another shot at the Yankees. After going only three innings the day before, he insisted on Fohl allowing him to start the second game. It is a situation that the modern-day reader may find difficult to believe in an age where four- and five-day rest periods are regarded as almost mandatory and where American League pitchers are not even required to bat.

The New York starter was Waite Hoyt, and the Browns picked up single runs off him in the first and second innings. In the initial inning Tobin walked, Gerber sacrificed him to second, and Sisler brought him home with the first of his three hits for the day. In the second Frank Ellerbe walked, went to second on a passed ball and then to third as Yankee catcher Al Devormer threw wildly. McManus's double then scored "Gov." But New York had gotten two runs of their own in the top of the second and three more in the fifth. Tobin drew the Browns closer at 5–4 by hitting a two-run homer in the fifth, but it would be as close as the team would get. The Yankees got three more runs off Shocker in the seventh when they put together a walk, three hits, and Ken Williams' throwing error to make the final score 8–4. Frank Baker, despite his Saturday injury, started the game at third for New York, but gave way to Mike McNally in the fifth inning after collecting a double in three trips to the plate, scoring a run, and making two assists in the field.

> Southpaw "Shucks" Pruett went to the hill this afternoon in the third game of the series with the Yankees in an effort to accomplish what Shocker had failed twice to do. It was Ladies Day and the female of the species demonstrated that it was just as foolish as the male. There were 10,000 women present and the overflow filled the temporary seats in front of both pavilions. The only unoccupied seats were

in the sun baked bleachers. About 14,000 persons were present.

So began the *Post-Dispatch*'s J. Roy Stockton in his story of the Monday game. In that contest, Fohl not only went to Pruett, who had suddenly become an effective starter, but replaced the slumping Jacobson with Shorten in center field and moved McManus up to Jacobson's fifth place in the batting order.

Pruett gave the Yankees only six hits, and while the New York starter, "Bullet Joe" Bush, surrendered only three more, among these were home runs to Ken Williams and John Tobin. Williams settled matters early by hitting number 15 in the bottom of the first for an early 2–0 lead. The Browns added another in the sixth and four more in the eighth for the 7–1 victory. But the day belonged to Pruett, who struck out Ruth three times. Such a performance was most appropriate for an L. C. Davis poem called "Leave It to Shucks":

There was a young fellow named Pruett
Who was a great pitcher and knew it
This scintillant youth
Humbled George Herman Ruth
When other great stars failed to do it.

In his route-going effort the young medical student walked only two – one of these was Ruth for his only on-base appearance of the game – and struck out three others in addition to Ruth. One of his called strikes caused an incident in the third inning when Yankee coach O'Leary objected too vehemently while Bush, who was an excellent hitter, was at bat. O'Leary was thrown out of the game and Bush singled, but nothing came of it as the next batter grounded into a double play.

The final game of the series on Tuesday, June 13, closely resembled the last game of the earlier St. Louis-New York series at the Polo Grounds. The Browns needed the victory for a split in the set and to retain the same distance in the pennant race that existed at the start. That being the case, the Browns went out and won the game as big as they had done a few weeks earlier. Fohl started Danforth, who like Pruett was being relied on as a dependable starter. Yankee manager Miller Huggins went with Bob Shawkey.

The club went to work on Shawkey with an early vengeance. Tobin led off with a single to center, Gerber walked, and Sisler singled past Aaron Ward at second. Tobin was thrown out at home trying to score from second, but it hardly mattered as McManus, after Williams went out, singled in Gerber and Sisler. Meusel misplayed the McManus hit, which went all the way to third, where Shorten doubled him home. Severeid then delivered the fourth run with his pop fly double to center.

New York resorted to a war of nerves as the battle on the diamond wasn't going to their liking. In the second inning the visitors protested to umpire Billy Evans that Danforth was marking the surface of the ball with his thumbnail. The game was frequently interrupted as Evans examined the balls, but he could find no reason to take any action against the St. Louis pitcher. Evans did retain and send to American League President Ban Johnson one ball which supposedly had "loaded" seams. Evans said that this ball may have acquired its dirt-filled seam by accident. Johnson took no action against Danforth at this time.

John Tobin's brother Jim recalls the controversy surrounding Danforth:

> He had a grip out of this world on that hand of his. I think he could almost prick the skin on a baseball.... Of course, whether he did anything I don't know, but he could squeeze it around.... They did quite a bit [of complaining about doctoring the ball], they never did get anything on [him], but I think it probably got to him nervouswise, getting nervous, everybody checking every time he threw the ball ... a good southpaw.

Though the Yankees made it close at 4–3 after four innings Danforth didn't let them bother him as his teammates drove Shawkey from the mound in the fifth. With one out, Sisler beat out an infield hit to Ward at second, who threw wildly to first, allowing him to take second. Williams then walked and McManus tripled them both home. Shorten, who was having a great time as Jacobson's replacement, singled to bring in the Browns' seventh run. Huggins didn't have to pull Shawkey. The New York ace simply walked from the mound at this point and George Murray, foregoing the formality of a warm-up, finally retired the side.

If Murray seemed effective in the fifth the illusion was quickly dispelled in the sixth when Fohl's men came up with five more runs. The feature of this rally was George Sisler's bases-loaded triple. Huggins relieved with "Lefty" O'Doul at this point, but the Browns came up with two more runs before the inning was over. Both teams later added an additional run, the Browns' tally coming as a result of Ruth's muff of Tobin's fly followed by Sisler's triple. The series, which had started so well for Ruth, in the first two games, ended with the Babe going zero for six in the last two games in addition to this run-producing error. The final score was 13–4 for St. Louis.

The clash between the major contenders had once again ended in a draw, though concluding most positively for the Browns. The Yankees went on to face Detroit while Washington invaded Sportsman's Park. Bayne started, but was quickly chased as the Senators built up a 5–0 lead over the first five innings. However, the explosiveness of the last New York game reappeared with a vengeance in the Browns' sixth when George Sisler homered with the bases loaded. L. C. Davis noted in "The Psychological Swat":

> With three men on and two men out
> The Browns three runs behind
> George Sisler made a home run clout
> Which seems to prove beyond a doubt
> He has a psychic mind
>
> The final score was seven-six
> In favor of the Browns
> In all the bag of baseball tricks
> There's nothing like those four base licks
> For chasing Fortune's frowns

The one-man pitching staff, Urban Shocker. The veteran spit-baller won 24 and lost 17 in 1922. (Photo courtesy of the *St. Louis Post-Dispatch.*)

Pruett picked up the victory in relief, blanking the "Griffs," as Washington was sometimes called after their owner, over the last three innings.

On June 15 Davis went the route as the club won again on McManus' home run 3–2. In a blow that would today be a ground rule double, the Browns' second baseman drove a ball to deep left field which hit the ground and then leaped over the fence. Davis gave up only six hits and did not walk a batter as Jacobson returned to the lineup. The news on the field continued good the following day: Vangilder finally regained his form with a nine-hit effort as the batters came up with eighteen hits and a 15–2 victory. Among the numerous hits were Williams' sixteenth home run and another by Marty McManus.

The *Sporting News* was particularly pleased with the Davis and Vangilder efforts:

> Davis, who certainly couldn't expect any compliments on his previous efforts, went to the box Wednesday and pitched not only one of the best best games of his career, but one of the most remarkable, for he didn't give a base on balls. Vangilder, who surely doesn't think he ought to be hailed as a king bee for what he has been doing for a month, set out to make his critics take it all back in the Thursday game. So keen was he that he pitched better ball than he had to, for the Browns gave him 15 runs to win on, and there have been few times when he has pitched better ball. This pair, therefore, having shown they can do it, we will leave it up to them to explain why then they don't.

While the victory sent the Browns into first place as the Yankees lost their third straight to Detroit, the joy was tempered with the announcement that the team's "meal card," Urban Shocker, had been admitted to a St. Louis hospital for treatment of a leg injury. The leg had been bothering him all season and after the second Yankee game of the recent series Shocker had publicly complained about his condition. The *Post-Dispatch* quoted Bob Quinn: "Of course we'll miss Shocker, but if we have a one pitcher ball club it is time to find it out. It is not right for a man to hobble around on an injured leg and so Shocker will stay in the hospital until he recovers." The original prognosis was that the righthander would be out only ten days, but it was to be July 4 before he would return.

Shocker had broken into organized baseball in 1913 with

Windsor, Ontario, of the Border League. Originally a catcher, he quickly found his niche on the mound and moved on to Ottawa of the Canadian League for the 1914 season. In 1915 he was purchased by the New York Yankees and compiled a 4-3 record the following season, splitting the year between New York and Toronto. By 1917 he had cracked the regular rotation and finished with an 8-5 slate. The Browns obtained him in 1918 for $15,000 and Del Pratt and Eddie Plank. It was in St. Louis that he enjoyed his greatest success, compiling season records of 6-5, 1918; 13-11, 1919; 20-10, 1920; and 27-12, 1921. The ex–Yankee was the unquestioned leader of the Browns pitching staff and one of a handful of major league pitchers permitted to use the spitball after it was outlawed in 1920.

Frank Ellerbe remembered him well as "one of the best." When asked if Shocker worked on the ball, Ellerbe responded:

> No, no, except he was one of the last spitball pitchers in the league.... He had control. He had the best control of that spitball of anybody I ever saw. He was a little wild, not wild with his pitching, but a little wild in his living. When he wasn't pitching someday maybe he might not show up, suppose to get four days rest. But he'd come back in the club house [and say], "Give me one today, boys, one run today and I'll beat 'em." Sometimes he'd come in and say, "Well I might need two, give me two runs and I'll beat em." And he came dang near doing it too, he won about 24 games, I think, that year. Best fielding pitcher I ever saw.... He could field that position, he'd leave that mound and jump on that ball like a cat.... If there was a man on second and they were putting [sacrificing] him over, he'd say: "Stay back, Gov, stay back. I'll get it." ... You'd see a slow one down the third base line, a bunt or sacrifice or anything, and if that runner from second would come, he'd jump on that ball and we'd cut him off at third ... and if the man didn't come he'd jump on that ball and we'd get him at first. He could really field his position.

Jim Tobin has briefer memories more related to Shocker's off-the-field activities: "I think he flew pretty high every once in awhile.... Urban Shocker used to be pretty well faced all the time. I don't know what it was from, but it would flush up real red...."

The series with Washington closed on June 17 with a 6–2 defeat, but the club retained first place as the Yankees lost again to Detroit. Danforth came up with a poor effort over the first seven innings, giving up ten hits and five walks as Tobin, Gerber, and Ellerbe all made errors. Pruett pitched the last two innings and was touched for the final two runs, both unearned.

Meanwhile the Browns' front office was experiencing the results of the team's rise to first place. World Series ticket orders started to inundate Bob Quinn's office! Quinn was pleased, but practical. The *Post-Dispatch* quoted him this way:

> It is far too early to consider seating arrangements for a World Series. Of course, we are all optimistic and eager to win, but there are still three and one half months of the season remaining.
>
> We will not accept any checks nor give any priority to requests for seats at this time. We have returned large numbers of them and will continue to do so until the arrival of an appropriate time for making seating arrangements.
>
> If we do have a series here we intend to sell the seats in small blocks only.

The major leagues' weekly Saturday release of statistics revealed that George Sisler was first in both leagues in the following departments; batting average (.439), runs scored (55); total hits (100), total bases, triples, and stolen bases (24). In addition he was the first player in either league to reach 100 hits and was close to the top in doubles and home runs in the American League. Ken Williams was the major league home run leader with 16, while Shocker was the winningest pitcher with a 12-7 record. The team was second in double plays in the American League with 54 while leading both leagues in runs scored with 331.

The Philadelphia Athletics played their first visit of the season on June 18 as "Dixie" Davis tried to continue his winning ways. The Browns won, but Davis didn't; Wayne Wright picked up the victory with his middle-inning relief work. Williams got number 17 and the team moved up one and a half games on New York as the Yankees lost to Cleveland. Good things continued the next day with another victory coupled with a New York loss. Fohl started Ray Kolp, who had seen relatively light service to this point, and he responded with a six-hit, route-going 3–2 victory. The winning run was scored in this rain-delayed game when McManus singled in Tobin from second. Tobin had reached second on Athletics shortstop Chick Galloway's error and Gerber's sacrifice. The Browns were now two and one-half games ahead of New York.

Vangilder won the third game of the set, scattering eight hits while pitching a complete game. Williams hit his eighteenth in the fifth inning with George Sisler on base to account for two of the St. Louis runs in the 7–3 win. Meanwhile in Cleveland not only were the Yankees losing, but Ruth was slapped with another suspension for using abusive language toward umpire Bill Dinneen. Dinneen had ejected Ruth from the prior day's game and league president Ban Johnson had set him down for three days. Prior to the June 20 game with the Indians the Babe had had a near confrontation with Dinneen, but Cleveland manager Tris Speaker and some of his players had intervened to prevent any trouble.

Ruth's suspension was his fourth of a season which was still not to the halfway point. His problems reflected a Yankee team torn by dissension and suffering from a lack of discipline. Robert Creamer's *Babe: The Legend Comes to Life* describes the 1922 Yankees:

> The players, [a] rowdy, independent group of drinkers, gamblers and wenchers – most of them, anyway – raised hell every night. Poker games went on until dawn. Empty bottles of bootleg liquor piled up in the halls. Some players were never in their own rooms all night. Huggins [a small man] looked littler than ever trying to control his wilful troupe. He had troubles with his players all year. He fined Mays in spring training, and he and the pitcher had a loud shouting

argument about that in the streets of Norfolk, Virginia. In May the hotheaded Hoyt, resenting Huggins' directions on how to pitch to a certain batter, blew up, lost a tight ballgame and got into a scrap with Huggins on the bench. Reports said Hoyt punched Huggins, but the pitcher said all he did was grab the manager's shoulder to turn him around. Huggins did not fine Hoyt, but in any case discipline was lacking.

Sid Mercer, a former Browns traveling secretary, now writing baseball for a New York newspaper, had his own thoughts on the Yankees' problems. In a piece prepared for the *Post-Dispatch* Mercer commented:

> There is nothing the matter with the Yankees except that Ruth is not hitting; neither are the other sluggers except Bob Meusel. Likewise the pitchers are not piching. Outside of that they look great. The answer to their temporary collapse is found in the pitching returns since they lost their first game in St. Louis a week ago Monday.
>
> In the eight consecutive games the Yanks have lost, the pitchers have been slammed for 104 hits, an average of 13 per game, and the enemy has scored 59 runs, an average of nearly eight per game.

Connie Mack sent his pitching ace, for that matter his only real pitcher, Eddie Rommel, to the hill for the final game of the series. Rommel averted a Browns sweep by giving up only four hits in the 5–0 shutout win. The Athletics pounded starter Wayne "Rasty" Wright and reliefer Dave Danforth for eleven hits. Only Tobin, Sisler, Jacobson, and Collins hit safely. The latter replaced Hank Severeid in the first inning when he was hit on the hand with a bat.

The chunky Collins caught the opening game in Detroit as the team began a brief road swing on June 22. Frank Ellerbe recalled that Hank Severeid was always fearful of someone taking his place permanently, and he no doubt watched the game uneasily from the dugout. It was an uneasy game to watch as Detroit started Howard Ehmke matched Pruett over eleven innings.

Finally in the Detroit eleventh shortstop Frank Rigney singled home George Cutshaw with the winning run in the 3–2 victory. Severeid watched again the following day as the Tigers made it two in a row over the Browns 10–6. Bayne was bombed out early and Kolp could not contain Detroit after taking over in the second and going into the fifth with a 5–4 lead. But Cobb's men came up with six more runs featured by Harry Heilmann's home run. Collins homered for St. Louis to add to Severeid's nervousness.

But the Story City, Iowa, native had no reason for concern as he went behind the bat for the Saturday game of the series. The Browns had lost three in a row, and Fohl selected Elam Vangilder to start the next game. Vangilder pitched well enough and carried a 7–3 lead after five innings. Fohl felt Vangilder was weakening and brought on Danforth to pitch in the sixth inning. With the bases loaded and Cobb the batter, a new riot broke out. The *Post-Dispatch*'s Dent McSkimming, now covering the Browns on the paper's rotation system, relates the incident:

> In the sixth inning the lid blew off and 50 policemen were required to quell a most interesting riot at the Browns' dugout.
>
> There were numerous contributory causes for the demonstration at the pit. One of them was that the Browns were winning. The immediate cause was the fact that Jimmy Austin threw Lou Blue's first baseman's mitt into the grandstand, not at anyone, particularly, but just to get it away from Haney, the Tiger player who was coaching at first. [This was the same Fred Haney who was later to manage the Browns, Pittsburgh, and Milwaukee, but was now in his rookie major league season.] Haney had resorted to tactics designed to disconcert Dave Danforth, who was pitching to Cobb. He tossed Blue's glove high into the air every time Dave prepared to deliver a pitch.
>
> Austin [a playing coach, it will be recalled] watched the performance until it chafed and then he ran out and grabbed the glove, just as Cobb was swinging wide at a third strike. Jimmy, in his enthusiasm, tossed the glove in the air a la Haney, and it landed in the grandstand.
>
> Forthwith fans, ball players and everybody else that cared

> to, piled into the Browns' dugout, evidently after Austin. Strange to relate Ty Cobb was not in the vanguard of the rioting party. He was busy examining the ball which Danforth had used to strike him out with the bases loaded. Docile Lee Fohl found himself pinioned on either side by two of "Detroit's finest." It took five minutes for the police to restore order. The umpires couldn't find anything wrong with any player's conduct, so no one was expelled. The game went on, the fans raving more wildly than ever....

The Browns added six more runs before the day was out to make the final 13–4 and bring the losing streak to an end. The victory put the team three games ahead of the Yankees, the longest lead they had held to this point.

Davis continued the good work on June 25 with a four-hit, 5–0 shutout. Ken Williams failed to collect a homer or for that matter a hit, but was brilliant in the field with a shoestring catch in the fifth and an over-the-shoulder catch in the eighth.

With the Browns riding high in first place the *Post-Dispatch* thought it appropriate to run a photograph of manager Lee Fohl with the caption "The Next Miracle Man?" The paper went on to comment that during the early stages of the 1921 season many were calling for Fohl's dismissal and Phil Ball responded by signing him for 1922. Ball was applauded for his perceptive judgment. The comment was made of Fohl that "he gives his players much latitude for exercising their own discretion and ... he has only three or four signals he employs from the bench."

Fohl was not the only one to be singled out for praise by the media as coach Jimmy Austin was praised by the *Sporting News* for his role in the Haney incident in Detroit. The baseball weekly said: "Jim's disturbance doesn't show in the box score, but it was effective. He waked up Tom Connolly, umpire, to a realization that an opposing team has rights when playing against Detroit...."

Austin was at the tail end of a journeyman's baseball career in 1922. The son of a Welsh shipbuilder, he had come to the United States at an early age and the family settled in Cleveland. After four minor league seasons he was sold to the New York Yankees, then called the Highlanders, before eventually moving to the Browns in 1911. He held down the regular third baseman's job until 1919 before tailing off to a reserve status and then eventually becoming a coach. Austin managed the Browns for part of the 1913 season and would later do the same on two other occasions. When Branch Rickey was still with the club he served as Rickey's "Sunday" manager. Rickey had promised his devout Methodist parents that he would never go to the ball park on a Sunday. Hence, someone was needed to manage the team on those days. Austin was "it" with the Browns. The practice continued when Rickey moved over to the Cardinals.

Austin had gained the reputation as something of a comedian. Dorothy Tobin recalled him: ". . . and, of course, old Jimmy Austin, the clown of the team. I can remember right as a kid I used to go out there . . . and it was just a lot of fun watching Jimmy Austin." Jim Tobin also remembered: "Yeah, he was always laughing and joshing around quite a bit." Jim said Austin played a lot of tricks on the other players. "He'd ride them once in a while."

Austin himself reminisced with Lawrence Ritter in conjunction with a chapter in Ritter's *The Glory of Their Times*:

> It turned out, though, that it was a big break for me, him [New York manager Hal Chase] trading me to the Browns like that. Because I stayed there for over 20 years, as a player until 1922 and as a coach for ten more years after that. When I went to St. Louis in 1911 the Browns were "the"team in that town, you know. It wasn't until the late twenties and thirties that the Cardinals became the big team in St. Louis. . . .
>
> Just think of me, a third baseman, playing most of my years throwing over to either Hal Chase [at New York] or George Sisler at first base. Why, that's heaven for a third baseman. There's no doubt that they were the two greatest fielding first baseman who ever lived and that's in anybody's book.
>
> Of the two, I guess I'd have to say that Chase was the better fielder. In a way I hate to say that, but you have to give the devil his due. Sis was a better all-around ballplayer. He started with us as a pitcher, you know. I was at third base

> one day in 1915 when he outpitched Walter Johnson and beat him 2–1. And, of course, Sis was a better hitter, one of the best of all time. But just on fielding alone, I'm afraid I'd have to pick Chase.

Pruett's string of successes ended when Cleveland beat him 6–0 on June 26 as the Browns opened a three-game series before returning to St. Louis. While Frank Ellerbe's fielding was outstanding, the team could get only five singles and a double off Cleveland starter Stan Coveleskie. With rain threatening, Fohl started Wayne Wright in the second game; after seven innings, with the rain now coming down quite heavily, the Browns led 7–3. But Cleveland exploded for six runs in the eighth, featuring Jamieson's bases-loaded triple, and went on to a 9–7 win. Neither Vangilder nor Danforth could stem the tide in relief. But the series finale was a solid 9–0 victory in which Ray Kolp continued his development as a solid starter by giving the Indians only four singles. St. Louis raked four Cleveland pitchers for fourteen hits; Bill Jacobson and Ken Williams collected three hits each. Cleveland first baseman "Stuffy" McInnis had recently completed a long errorless playing streak, eventually winding up with 163 consecutive games without a miscue. The *Post-Dispatch*'s Dent McSkimming observed:

> The quite natural tendency of the Cleveland official scorer to favor the infallible "Stuffy" McInnis was illustrated in this round [fifth inning]. With Sisler on first and two out, Jamieson lifted a fly to short right. McInnis went back to get the ball over his head and muffed it. Sisler rounded third and Jacobson dashed for second. McInnis recovered the ball and pegged to second, but the ball went into the bag on a bounce and [shortstop] Swell muffed it, Sisler scoring.
>
> Jacobson was credited with a single and Sewell, who muffed McInnis' bad throw, was charged with an error. The infallible McInnis got by without any damage to his spotless record.

The Browns returned to St. Louis to face these same Indians

on June 30 as they began a brief home stand before launching their second Eastern invasion. Vangilder came through with a solid nine-inning effort, and the club raked two Cleveland pitchers for 12 hits en route to a 10–3 victory. Shorten contributed a home run. The victory solidified the St. Louis hold on first place by three games over New York as the season approached its midpoint.

5

JULY

"I Never Doctored the Ball"

July began as optimistically as June, with the club leading the league and continuing their domination over Cleveland. Fohl sent Wayne Wright to the hill on July 1, and he responded with a four-hitter in the 4–3 win. The game marked the third straight complete game performance by a Browns pitcher and featured some outstanding outfield play by Ken Williams and "Baby Doll" Jacobson. The *Post-Dispatch* now had J. Roy Stockton on the Browns beat, and he observed of Jacobson:

> In the adjoining meadow was William Jacobson, a lumbering Swede from Moline, Ill. William, or Bill or Jake or "Baby Doll" as the lumbering one is known, does not look like a great outfielder. If you entered a hotel lobby and saw Jake among the ball players you would never guess that he was a brilliant outfielder. But he is a great outfielder and yesterday he shone with the brilliance of a champion. He had not the grace of Williams, nor the speed, apparently, but he was just as efficient. Time and again balls lined toward center which appeared certain to fall safe. But only once did one of them fall safe near Jake. Seven times he made his catch. He roved to right and he ranged toward left, he galloped in behind second and romped back to the shadow of the flagpole to haul down tremendous wallops.

William Chester "Baby Doll" Jacobson hit .317 in 1922. (Photo courtesy of Carita Jacobson Johnson.)

Jacobson was born in Cable, Illinois, on August 16, 1890, and began his professional career in 1909 with Rock Island in the Three I League. He played in only 48 games that year, batting but .185. He saw even less action the next year before being sent to Battle Creek in the Southern Michigan League, where he hit .233 in 55 games. The next year it was back to Rock Island, only this time he recorded the first of many .300 average seasons, coming in with a .311 mark. From there it was on to excellent seasons in the Southern Association with Mobile and Chattanooga before arriving in the majors with Detroit in 1915. But it was at Mobile that he gained his famous nickname. Jacobson later related how he came to be known as "Baby Doll" to Murray Hurt, sports editor of the *Rock Island Argus*:

> I was the property of the New York Giants at that time. We were working our way North after spring training and the club stopped off at Mobile for a Sunday exhibition game. John McGraw, the Giants manager, decided to leave three of us there for the season, so on Wednesday of the same week, we were in Mobile for Opening Day.
>
> They had a band playing on the field, and just before the first pitch, they played "Oh, You Beautiful Doll." And just a couple of minutes later, I led off the home first and hit the first pitch over the fence. A lady behind home plate stood up just as I finished circling the bases and yelled: "That must be that Beautiful Baby Doll they were just talking about." Well from that day to this, I've been Baby Doll. Most people never knew my given name was Bill.

With the Tigers, "Jake," as most players referred to him, found himself playing behind Ty Cobb and Sam Crawford, both of whom eventually found their way to Cooperstown, and .300-hitting Bobby Veach. Then on August 18 he was traded to the Browns. His performance in St. Louis was such that he was back in the Southern Association with Little Rock for the 1916 season. He proceeded to lead the league in hitting with a .346 average and finish first in hits (176) and triples (15). With that record, a virtual repeat of his 1914 season with Chattanooga, Jacobson returned to St. Louis to stay in 1917. After spending 1918 in World War I service with the Navy he came back to hit .323, following this with .355 in 1920 and .352 in 1921. By the time 1922 arrived the combination of Jacobson, Williams, and Tobin formed one of the greatest hitting outfields ever assembled on one team.

John McGraw would later say of Jacobson:

> One of the most determined players I ever saw was "Baby Doll" Jacobson. . . . He is a giant (6′ 2½″, 210) in stature and always was a good hitter. For a big man he is rather fast on the bases. He was a very poor slider though, at first.
>
> It was tough on a big fellow like him to hit the sand with his whole weight, but he stuck to it for hours at a time. Not once did I ever hear him whimper. In time he got where he could do the hook slide as well as any of them.

Ray Kolp continued the complete game trend on July 2 as Ken Williams hit home run number 20, scoring Sisler and McManus ahead of him. Cleveland got to Kolp for four runs in the eighth before hanging on for a 9–5 victory. An incident in this inning reveals an interesting umpire reversal at the expense of the Browns. The *Post-Dispatch*'s Joseph Holland reported:

> In this inning there were two out, one run was in and Speaker was on third when McInnis cut a slow roller to short. Gerber rushed in on the ball and lined it to Sisler who stretched far to the right field side of the base for the catch. Umpire Chill waved McInnis out and the Browns went to their dugout, and the Indians, with the exception of Speaker, started for their positions in the field.
>
> Speaker went to first and by some powerful vocal play, succeeded in having Chill submit his verdict at first to Tom Connolly for review. Tom took the appeal and reversed the decision and remanded McInnis to first and allowed Speaker to score. [It might be remembered here that Chill was the umpire involved in the Browns' famous come-from-behind 8–2 victory against New York on May 20.] Of course, Lee Fohl protested vigorously, but one reversal was all that an umpire's reputation could stand on one play.

> Chill was standing right at first base when he decided the play while Connolly, at the plate, was 60 feet distant. Chill explained after the game that first base was so blackened with mud that he could not be sure that Sisler's shoe was in contact with it at the time he caught the ball, so he appealed to Connolly 80 feet further away and looking through a mask, to straighten it out for him.

Monday, July 3, was a travel day: The Browns hopped the train for Chicago and a traditional July 4 doubleheader before beginning their Eastern swing in Boston. The two games would mark the return of Urban Shocker to the active roster after three weeks. During his absence the supposedly "no name" staff had compiled a record of 11–5 and had kept a firm grip on the top of the American League. But now it was time for the master once again to assume his natural role.

Fohl chose to use Shocker initially in a relief role in both ends of the Chicago doubleheader. Pruett started the morning game, but his wildness brought him to grief in the fifth inning and Fohl signaled to Shocker to come to the rescue. But the old magic was not quite back yet. He walked in the tying run that Pruett had put on base and later gave up two more runs for the White Sox to win 5–3. It took the afternoon game to reveal the "old" Shocker. Danforth had started the game and carried a 5–3 lead into the Chicago ninth. Sheely led off for the White Sox with a double, and Danforth delivered two balls to catcher Ray Schalk before Fohl decided for the second time that day to go to Shocker. He responded by striking out pinch-hitter Amos Strunk, batting for the "other" Urban, opposing pitcher Faber. Severeid then nailed Sheely attempting to steal third, and shortstop Johnson was retired on a fly ball to Ken Williams. End of game – and a "save" for Shocker in an era when such statistics were not commonly kept.

Later, from the train to Boston, the *Post-Dispatch*'s J. Roy Stockton quoted Shocker on his return:

> Oh, boy! It certainly did feel good to bear down on that old right leg and not have pain shoot through the limb. That's

> the first time since early spring that I have been able to pitch without it hurting me, and now all I need now is a little hard work. I'll be a winning pitcher again soon.

Ironically, in the same edition in which the above quote appeared there was an advertisement for Merrell's Penetrating Oil with enthusiastic endorsements from both Shocker and Ken Williams. While not claiming that the oil was responsible for his recovery, Shocker did have this to say about the oil: "I cannot speak too highly of this powerful liniment, and heartily recommend it to all professional and amateur players. It sure does keep one's arm in first class shape, and I don't think a pitcher should be without it."

How much Shocker and Williams received for their endorsement is not known, but one suspects not very much even by 1922 standards. A proposal made the same year to "Baby Doll" Jacobson gives us an idea of what kind of offers were made to players in this era before the player agent.

The following letter was on the letterhead of the Baseball Magazine Company:

> Dear Mr. Jacobson:
>
> You have a chance to do me a favor and at the same time get something for yourself. The Tobacco Products Corp. of N.Y. are planning to bring out a new brand of cigarettes. We will be able to sell them some advertising which we very much need, with your cooperation. Here is the plan.
>
> They want your permission to insert your picture (which we will print for them) in some of their cigarette packages. In return for your permission, they will send you by return mail 2,000 CIGARETTES worth $40.00. Will you please sign the attached blank and return in the enclosed stamped envelope? Thanking you for this favor and wishing you the best of luck, I am
>
> Sincerely yours,
>
> F. C. Lare
> Editor

As the Browns sped eastward there was speculation that the possibility of a nationwide railroad strike might play havoc with the schedule. Traveling Secretary Willis Johnson indicated that should that possibility become reality there were plans to hold the Browns and other western clubs in the East for two series rather than one and then revise the schedule accordingly. In the East the distances between cities was short and the trips could be made by auto or boat. Fortunately, the strike was settled in such time as to prevent these contingency plans from being implemented.

The club came into Boston with a game shaved off their previous three-game edge, facing the prospect of having to play three doubleheaders in three days, and carrying team vice president Walter Fritsch along for the ride. But Fritsch would do more than merely travel with the team. The arduous schedule of the doubleheaders had been made possible by previous rainouts and came just prior to a critical four-game series with the Yankees beginning on July 11. To further compound difficulties Boston owner Harry Frazee postponed the July 6 doubleheader for no apparent reason. The *Post-Dispatch*'s J. Roy Stockton reported that "no umpire in any league would have called off the scheduled doubleheader yesterday.... But despite the bright sun that had the field in a near dusty condition by 3 o'clock, the Browns floated about the town and accumulated grouches."

Fritsch was furious. Stockton quoted him:

> Frazee's purpose is too obvious to need pointing out. We go to New York after this series and three doubleheaders in three days, even if there is an open Sunday date, will send us to the Polo Grounds with our pitching staff overworked. I am certain that Frazee postponed the games today deliberately to aid the Yankees. The deals between the two clubs, financial and as to players, in the past two years, show how closely these two club owners are united.

The team vice president was not content with a mere verbal blast, but had photographs taken of Fenway Park's field conditions on July 6 for later presentation at the major league meetings.

While providing no immediate respite from the situation at hand the rules were, of course, ultimately changed to place cancellations in the hands of the umpires rather than the club owners. In addition, the arbiters were allowed up to one hour prior to game time to make such a decision.

While Fritsch and Fohl were properly concerned with the impact of three consecutive doubleheaders or the pitching staff, the *Sporting News* in a relatively rare commendation to any Browns pitcher other than Shocker commented:

> Today Lee Fohl has a surplus of superior pitching... Whatever came over those pitchers of the Browns we don't know. It may have been they only needed the right sort of a chance; it may be the crippling of Shocker aroused them to the needs of the team, or maybe a few harpoons sunk into their hides made them rare up and go – but at any rate they are going....

The level of pitching continued at a high level, but unfortunately the Browns' luck did not. The three doubleheaders were split with the losses all being by one run. Two of the six games went into extra innings with the clubs each taking one. Fohl gave Shocker his first start in the opener on July 7 and the effort was typical of the star righthander: a complete game and shutout as the Browns got the only run they needed in the third inning. Ken Williams was ejected in the sixth for protesting a called third strike and sat out the second game as well. The latter was to be the only game in which Williams would not appear during 1922. "Chick" Shorten took his place. The second game went thirteen innings and ended when Pruett, who had been running a long bad string, gave up a home run to Boston first baseman George Burns for the 5–4 loss.

Vangilder started the opener on July 8 and gave up only two hits and one run going into the Boston ninth. A superb effort, but not quite enough as former Brown Del Pratt tripled in George Burns with the winning run and a 2–1 loss. The Browns had collected eight hits and George Sisler had swiped three bases, but all for naught. The hitting came at the right time in the second game as the club got fourteen and a resulting ten runs. Ray Kolp started the game, but weakened in the late innings; this time, however, Pruett was effective in stemming the Red Sox momentum.

The final doubleheader began with another thirteen-inning affair, but this time St. Louis was the victor by the same 5–4 score with which Boston had triumphed two days earlier. "Dixie" Davis (a noted long-inning hurler, it will be remembered) pitched to all but one batter in collecting the victory. Once again Fohl used Pruett in relief. The Browns won the game when Frank Ellerbe squeezed in Bill Jacobson from third. Eddie Foster, who was to play a key role for the Browns later in the season, was used as a pinch-hitter by Boston, but Pruett retired him for the last out. In the last game Danforth started and was relieved by Wright in the seventh trailing 4–2. The club got one run in the ninth and narrowly missed tying the game when Sisler was thrown out on a close play at first for the last out of the game as Tobin was crossing the plate with what would have been run number four.

The Browns headed for New York with a game-and-a-half lead over the Yankees and the prospect of not having their starting third baseman, Frank "Governor" Ellerbe, available for the key four-game set. Ellerbe had injured his knee in the Boston series, an injury which would prove fatal to his career as he appeared in only a handful of games for the remainder of the season.

Frank Ellerbe was born in Marion County, South Carolina, the son of William H. Ellerbe, the governor of South Carolina, on Christmas Day 1895. The origin of Frank Ellerbe's nickname is obvious; yet, ironically, he never really knew his father as the latter died (in office) when the future Browns third baseman was only three years old.

The young Ellerbe developed into a fine athlete and enrolled at the University of the South (Sewanee), located near Nashville, Tennessee. He played both football and baseball there and later at Wofford College. He was good enough at both to be named

Frank Ellerbe held down the third base job until an old football injury to his knee sidelined him in July 1922. (Photo courtesy of the *St. Louis Post-Dispatch*.)

second team All-Southern halfback and first team All-Southern shortstop. Navy service in World War I then came along. After it was all over, Ellerbe was surprised to get a telegram from Clark Griffith, owner of the Washington Senators. It was an invitation to Washington and a chance to play major league baseball.

Ellerbe later told Eugene Fallon, sportswriter for the Florence, South Carolina, *Morning News*:

> You could have knocked me over with a feather. I had no idea that I'd been scouted by the Washington Senators.... You see, I'd never played anything but amateur baseball.... Did I want to play big league ball? Does a duck like water?

Ellerbe signed with Washington and Griffith sent him to Binghamton of the International League, but the young South Carolinian was soon playing as the regular third baseman in Washington. He stayed there until June 1921 when the Browns, desperately needing help at third base, traded Earl Smith, an outfielder they were attempting to make into a third baseman, to Washington for him. His arrival with the Browns prompted an interesting exchange on money matters which is particularly revealing today, with the modern-day emphasis on player rights. Ellerbe recalled:

> When I went to the Browns ... I never did like the Browns' ball park. In the first place the Browns and the Cardinals played together, they kept the infield cut to pieces all the time and it was hot as the devil there in St. Louis. I joined them in New York. I went over to the Ansonia Hotel. I told Lee Fohl I wouldn't get in uniform unless they paid me.... (I) asked for $1000.... He (Fohl) said: "I can't promise you that. You go ahead and get in uniform and play and I'll promise you the day we get back to St. Louis I'll go to the office and tell Bob Quinn what you want and try to get him to give you the $1000." ... I said, "All right I'll get in uniform and go out and play." And we went out in the Polo Grounds that day and as luck would have it I had a good day in the field and at bat. I got four for four. I haven't had four for four

> since! . . . Time we get back to St. Louis Lee Fohl did exactly what he said he'd do. He went up and talked to Quinn. Bob Quinn called me up there, He says: "You're holding us up here . . . terrible, we're not drawing much crowds, times hard." And I said: "Well, I won't play, I'll just go ahead and quit unless I can get the $1000 raise." . . . I told him if he'd give me the $1000 I'd go ahead and play with them. He says: "Gov, you're holding me up. Isn't your daddy governor of South Carolina?" I said: "No, Mr. Quinn, he was governor of South Carolina, but he died when I was three and one half years old. . . . He [Quinn] wanted me to write my daddy and ask him . . . if he [Ellerbe's father] was doing bad, holding them up like for the $1000 extra. . . . But then they hummed and hawed and talked a little bit and then he [Quinn] finally said: "Ok, I'll give you the $1000."

Ellerbe hit a solid .288 over the remainder of the 1921 season for St. Louis and started the season at third base. He played regularly there until the aggravation of an old knee injury in the Boston series. Ellerbe still remembers the injury and its aftermath:

> When I hurt my knee in Boston . . . when we jumped to New York, doctors in the Ansonia Hotel, they tried to give me ten days to two weeks rest and the knee would be alright. But for lack of reserve strength they put little Gene Robertson in there and he lost one game and they put old Herman Bronkie in and he was too old . . . ran in for an infield ball, he'd stumble all over his own feet. Lee Fohl got frantic, he wanted to win the pennant so bad. We jumped from New York down to Washington and with just three days rest he said: "Gov, you've got to get back in there!" I said: "Well, Lee, I can't jump around out there, this thing's liable to buck on me again." He said: "I'd rather have you out there and do the best you can." I went in anyway and Ray Kolp was pitching and their pitcher Francis was at bat, man on first and time for a bunt. I sort of eased up looking for Francis to bunt, as he bunted the ball I started to make my break for it and down I go, flat on my face. As luck would have it Francis bunted the ball up in the air and Ray Kolp ran and caught it and doubled the man off first. [This game was rained out before it became an official contest.]

As Ellerbe indicated, Fohl started rookie Gene Robertson at third base and, of course, Shocker pitched the first game against New York. The Browns took an early 1–0 lead, but bad luck and faulty fielding were to be their undoing. In the Yankee second, Aaron Ward hit a liner which Ken Williams leapt for only to have the ball bounce off his glove into the left field seats for a home run. With the score tied in the sixth Tobin committed two errors on the same play and allowed Ruth to hit an "unofficial" home run. The play was particularly costly as the run proved to be the margin of victory. Ruth lifted a high fly down the right field line which Tobin raced to catch, but dropped, allowing Ruth to take second. Only he didn't stop there. Ruth moved towards third and Tobin was taken by surprise. His throw to Robertson hit in front of him, took a bad hop, and went towards the stands as the Babe scored the winning run. Shocker had given up only seven hits, but it was not good enough. The Yankees beat him for the third time.

With New York now only a half-game behind, Fohl replaced Jacobson in center field with another rookie, Cedric Durst, while keeping Robertson at third and starting Ruth-killer "Shucks" Pruett. Jacobson had had a poor first game with two strikeouts and two groundouts, in addition to suffering from a lame leg.

St. Louis took an early 3–0 lead going into the fifth with the highlight being Ken Williams' twenty-first home run. In that inning another incident involving umpire Ollie Chill precipitated a fifteen-minute ruckus, which did not prevent the Yankees from tying the score. With two out and starting pitcher Waite Hoyt on third and Mike McNally at first, "Long Bob" Meusel singled to center off Pruett. Hoyt easily scored, but Durst made a bad throw to Robertson and the ball bounded into the Browns' dugout. McNally scored the second run, and Meusel came in with number three. The Browns argued vociferously that Chill had held up Meusel at third, but that the Yankee right fielder had ignored his signal and had come on in to score. The basis of the St. Louis complaint was the ground rule giving a runner two bases on a wild throw into the dugout. The *New York Times* recalls the scene:

> At once there was an uproar. Lee Fohl and the nine St. Louis players rushed at Umpire Ollie Chill and screamed in his face. Urban Shocker, Jimmy Austin, Lefty Leifield and a few others scurried out from the bench and flung themselves at the umpire. They raged and stormed, argued, pleaded and swore. They demanded that Meusel be sent back to third....
>
> Chill stood firm and Fohl led his gang to Connolly, umpiring behind the plate. The latter upheld his colleague, and the storm then whirled around his head. Making no headway here, half the mob went to see if Chill had suffered a change of heart. After ten minutes of wearisome debate Chill pulled his watch, but it must have stopped, for the conflagration went on for ten minutes more. Just when Fohl seemed to be through a fresh thought occurred to him. After fifteen minutes of it the umpires cleared the lot of the gang and the game went on.

But the problem with umpires did not end there. Only this time the incident involved the Yankees. As the sixth inning began New York manager Miller Huggins made a comment from the bench. Connolly told him to keep quiet or out he'd go. Huggins chose to ignore that advice and was thumbed out on his next utterance. The *New York Times* commented sarcastically: "One minute for Huggins, fifteen for Fohl."

The Browns broke the game open in the eighth on Sisler's bases-loaded single and a like hit by McManus. Four runs came in and the Browns won 7–4. Pruett needed relief help from Vangilder, who got the win, but the rookie lefthander kept up his domination of Babe Ruth. Ruth fanned three times, twice with the bases full and once with runners on second and third.

The rains came to New York on July 13 and that game was cancelled. It was then added to the three-game series scheduled for the Polo Grounds in late August. For the July 14 game Fohl pulled Robertson and elected to go with the aging veteran Herman Bronkie at third base while Jacobson returned to center field. Shocker, who had asked to pitch the first and last game of every New York series, was on the hill.

The Yankees once again pulled within a half-game of the Browns, getting to Shocker for four runs in the fourth inning and a final 4–0 victory. The ace righthander was in trouble from the start as New York threatened in the early innings before piling up five singles in the fourth. Pipp led off with the first single to right. After Ward went out with Pipp going to second, Scott scored the latter with the second single. With the hit and run-on, Schang got number three, sending Scott to third. Yankee pitcher Bob Shawkey, who gave the Browns but six hits, then sacrificed. Sisler came in and bobbled the ball, allowing Scott to score. Shocker recovered in time to get Shawkey at first, but Schang was now on second. Witt then got the fourth single and the third New York run scored. Witt then stole second and came in on the fifth single by Mike McNally.

Shocker gave up 12 hits before being relieved by Dave Danforth in the eighth. It was also one of George Sisler's rare bad games. Besides the play in the fourth noted above, he forced Tobin in the first, and then, after singling to open the fourth, Yankee catcher Schang caught him off first. In the sixth with two out and Tobin on third he flied out to end the inning. But as W. C. Fields would observe of him: "Well, even the perfect player can't have everything." Bronkie's play at third base drew this observation from the *New York Times*: "Herman didn't play the most alert game of the season."

Clinging to a scant half-game lead, the Browns continued their Eastern swing in Washington. As related previously, Fohl restored Ellerbe to the line-up and started Wright in the first game. Wright pitched well enough to win, allowing the Senators only six hits, but the Browns failed to get their eight hits in the right places and the result was a 2–0 defeat. The club had now gone nineteen straight innings without a run and had lost seven of their last twelve games. Nonetheless they kept their half-game lead as the Yankees lost in Chicago.

The slump was broken on July 16, when Davis gave Washington only five hits. Walter Johnson was the opposing pitcher, and the Browns got to him for nine hits and a 2–0 win. Fohl shook up his batting order for one of the relatively few times during the season by moving Gerber to the lead-off position and dropping Tobin to second. The *Post-Dispatch*'s J. Roy Stockton observed:

> Fohl has been told all over the circuit that Tobin gets too many hits to be wasted at the top of the list. If John had been lower in the list or if Gerber had been hitting, the St. Louis boy would be high in driving in runs. He has batted over .450 on the trip and right now is the most dangerous hitter among the Brownies.

The move paid immediate dividends as both Gerber and Tobin got two hits each and scored both St. Louis runs. Jacobson's batting slump continued though he ranged far and wide in the outfield for five put-outs, effectively stifling the Washington attack. Chicago again defeated New York, allowing the lead to increase to one and a half games.

Rain postponed the remaining two games of the series, and the Browns went on to Philadelphia for the opener there on July 19. The game was both an embarrassment and a disaster. Connie Mack started, for the first time in the majors, a raw rookie from the sandlots of Newark, New Jersey, Adolph Rettig. The rookie went the distance as Athletics power hitter Clarence "Tilly" Walker hit two home runs off Urban Shocker in the 6–3 triumph. Despite Ellerbe's experience in the Washington rainout, Fohl still started him, with the result that he once again wrenched his knee and had to be carried off the field. Bronkie finished for him. Still the lead held as the Yankees lost in Detroit.

Speculation grew around the American League that a deal would be made to strengthen the Browns' bench. Perhaps with Ellerbe's situation at hand and Jacobson's batting slump continuing, various possible trades were discussed in the press. A Washington writer had suspended White Sox pitcher Dick Kerr reinstated and in a St. Louis uniform. Another writer traded an unnamed outfielder and pitcher to Philadelphia for home run hitters "Tilly" Walker and "Bing" Miller. But as the *Post-Dispatch*'s J. Roy Stockton concluded:

> ...Fohl apparently is satisfied with his strength, both in the field and on the bench. Durst has substituted occasionally for Jacobson, but although the Texas youth is recognized as a brilliant prospect, he has not had the experience to be thrown into the breach with the championship at stake. He needs to ride the bench a bit longer.
>
> Shorten, the other utility outfielder, is a fine hitter, but lacks the speed that characterizes the work of Williams and Tobin, for whom he substitutes.
>
> Gene Robertson, Jimmie Austin and Herman Bronkie constitute the infield reserves. Robertson has played some brilliant and some unfortunate baseball, when substituting. He is a coming youngster and Bronkie is a going veteran. Bronkie did some good fielding in the pinch in the final at New York [it will be recalled that the *New York Times* disagreed], but did not get any hits. Austin, of course, can go in there any time and deliver, but his eyes cannot perform as well as his arm and hands.
>
> If no one is injured the team can scrape through very nicely. It won't need any breaks to win the pennant. If it plays up to its normal stride and hits as it can hit, part of the World Series will be played at Sportsman's Park. But if the hitting slump continues and Chicago keeps up its fast gait, first place will be hard to hold, and if Tobin or Williams or Sisler should be injured, it virtually would be fatal, doctor, fatal!

Vangilder proceeded to shut out Philadelphia in the second game 4–0, giving up only five hits. He was aided by four double plays, but the St. Louis attack could still muster only six hits with Jacobson getting three of these. But the slump was quickly a thing of the past when the club erupted for consecutive 10–2 and 10–1 victories in the final two games of the series. In the 10–2 game Sisler, McManus, and Bronkie (now Ellerbe's full-time replacement) each collected three hits of the Browns' total of sixteen, while Hank Severeid got his first home run of the year. "Rasty" Wright got the complete game win. The 10–1 game featured a home run by McManus and nineteen other hits. Those collecting at least three each were Gerber (still batting first), Tobin, Williams, and Jacobson. Every Brown got at least one hit and Ray Kolp the complete game victory. The lead was now two and a half games as the Yankees continued a slump of their own.

What brought about the sudden resurgence? It will be recalled that Walter Fritsch, the Browns' vice president, was making the trip. The *Post-Dispatch*'s J. Roy Stockton credits him with a "Cheer 'Em-Up Party" following the defeat in the first game of the Philadelphia series:

> He [Fritsch] called all the boys together and said they must forget baseball for a few hours. He brought cigarettes and mints and a few other things, took the boys to his suite of rooms and told them to sing, talk, and yell about anything but baseball. The first one that mentioned baseball, pennant, standing of the clubs, was to be kicked out of the room.
>
> Yesterday morning the mints were untouched, but the cigarettes and other things were gone. And there was that in the face of the Browns which had not been seen for a long time. They were smiling to themselves. There were funny stories and nobody thought of talking baseball. The result was that when they went out to the ball field they were fresh and keen for the conflict and their play was more peppery, more sparkling, more spontaneously brilliant than it had been for a month.... Lee Fohl was "in on" the evening. He told Fritsch after Wednesday's game that here was the time for him to give the boys the entertainment he had been talking about. Also a telegram was sent to Phil Ball telling him about the mints and a few other things and then the evening was on. Phil wired back that he "hoped the boys had gone to it" [and] that he felt like it himself.

After such a two-game attack Fohl was hopeful of concluding the road trip with a win in Detroit in a single game before the return to St. Louis. A win would give the team a 10–8 record for the trip as well as a positive start for the four-game set with the Yankees which would open the home stand.

If the Browns could have avoided the fourth and sixth innings they might have given Fohl what he wanted. But both those innings were five-run disasters and neither Davis, Pruett, Wright, Danforth nor Bayne was terribly effective. The defense was not much better, allowing seven errors. The Tigers won 11–6, though the Browns at one time held an early 5–0 lead. Umpires Owens and Connolly missed their train connections in Buffalo, and St. Louis trainer "Bitz" Bierhalter and his counterpart from Detroit, Howley, were pressed into service as arbiters. That fact precipitated an incident with Fred Haney, who, it will be recalled, was involved in the glove-throwing melee in Detroit the previous month. Haney was called out by Bierhalter at the plate in the fourth inning, and the Tiger rookie responded by throwing dirt in his face. Bierhalter, who sported a watermelon-sized paunch, swung a fist at Haney's face. Haney's teammates, pretending to be peacemakers, crowded around and stepped on Bierhalter's toes with their spikes!

On Monday, July 24, the Browns returned to St. Louis and to the biggest news of the season since Ruth's reinstatement. The Boston Red Sox, referred to by many as the Yankees' "big league farm club," continued the well-established shuttle service to New York by sending star third baseman Joe Dugan and outfielder Elmer Smith to the second-place club. The Yankees gave up "Chick" Fewster, a utility infielder-outfielder; Johnny Mitchell, utility infielder; and Elmer Miller, utility outfielder, as well as a pitcher to be named later. There were also unconfirmed rumors of cash being involved. Not one regular went to Boston for the player who was regarded as the premier third baseman in the league. The *Post-Dispatch*'s New York Bureau correctly reported the outcry that would result:

> The general feeling in baseball circles around the town last night, when the news became known, was that a grand roar may be expected from the other teams that are fighting the Yankees for the pennant and that the Yankee Colonels [owners Ruppert and Huston] are trying to "buy the championship." . . . There was a lot of talk about the "check book champions." Now a similar outburst may be expected and also some more of the attack on Frazee for "wrecking" the Red Sox.

The *Post-Dispatch*'s J. Roy Stockton commented:

> New York's expensive ball club, reinforced by the most recent purchase of Joe Dugan and Elmer Smith, will call at Sportsman's Park this afternoon to meet the Browns, their principal enemy and the one which made Cols. Ruppert and Huston realize that they had better be up and buying.

St. Louis fandom reacted as might be expected, with both the Chamber of Commerce and the Rotary Club sending letters of protest to Commissioner Landis and both league presidents. The Rotary Club letter follows:

> Dear Sir:
>
> Realizing that the best interest of baseball as the typical American sport will be best served by the adherence of those who control its affairs to the principles of true sportsmanship, the Rotary Club of St. Louis, composed of representative leaders in 250 lines of business addresses to you herewith a solemn protest against the recent "trade" between the New York and Boston American League clubs.
>
> We believe that the practice of allowing a strong major league club to strengthen itself at the expense of its rivals by purchasing the "stars" of a competing club in mid-season is indefensible. We believe that a continuation of this practice will militate against the future of baseball and that it will ultimately defeat its own ends by sacrificing public confidence.
>
> When one club is permitted to mortgage its future directly or indirectly to another club it leads to a condition of affairs not compatible with true sportsmanship.
>
> If the winning of pennants is to be only a matter of going out and buying up talent, the inevitable conclusion is that certain of the larger cities, New York in particular, will be given a false advantage by reason of its plentiful checkbook. The annual pennant chase will in time become a one team "race."
>
> Although the supposition is natural that we as citizens of St. Louis, are interested in the progress of the St. Louis teams in both leagues, we desire to here set forth our protest

> deeper, that we urge the adherence to those fundamentals of clean American sport that assure the constant and increasing growth of our national game.
>
> It is our hope that this protest will begin to bring about consideration of legislation by those in charge of the conduct of baseball's affairs that will prevent forever the repetition of such an unsportsmanlike "deal."
>
> We urge your earliest consideration of the foregoing.

As with the previous uproar concerning the cancellation of the doubleheader in Boston, this incident subsequently resulted in changing the deadline for trades to the present-day June 15 date. Players can still move to other teams after that date via the waiver route.

With the trade still very much on the minds of all St. Louis fans, some 18,000 of the faithful were on hand on July 25 as Shocker got the customary first call against New York. The Yankees had beaten their former teammate four times in a row, but that streak was about to come to an end, though not before a few anxious moments. Ironically, Dugan was the second batter up in the game and slammed one of Shocker's pitches for a double. He died there as Meusel struck out and Ruth grounded to Gerber. In the second Schang and Pipp singled putting men on first and third. After Ward struck out the stage was set for the type of spectacular defensive play that was one of George Sisler's trademarks. "Deacon" Scott attempted to squeeze Schang in from third, but in doing so popped the ball toward first. Sisler had anticipated the move by leaping high to make the put-out and then rifling the ball to Bronkie at third to get Schang for the double play.

The Browns broke through in the fourth when Williams hit number 22 with Sisler on for an early 2–0 lead. But in the sixth they hammered New York starter Carl Mays and reliefer "Lefty" O'Doul for five runs and six hits to take a 7–0 lead. But the *Post-Dispatch*'s J. Roy Stockton was forever wary of the Yankees: "For there is a constant threat in the bats of the Yankees. They have been brought from far and near by the bank rolls of the wealthy New York magnates, and there was no telling when the bats might begin functioning as they were bought to function."

There was no reason to fear in this case. St. Louis added a run in the eighth to make the final read 8–0 and the lead two and one-half games. It was in a sense a highwater mark of its own for the Browns in this memorable season. While the team would hold first place during portions of the remaining schedule, they were now 6-6 in the season series with the Yankees and would never come closer to equality with their rival.

"Rasty" Wright started the second game and gave the Yankees but one hit and one run for the first six innings. Weakening in the seventh, he gave up a two-run home run to Ruth, and Fohl brought in Danforth to pitch the eighth inning. The Browns had gotten five runs off starter Waite Hoyt and reliefer Joe Bush in their half of the seventh to carry an apparently safe 6–3 lead into the eighth. But neither Danforth nor Shocker nor Bayne could stem the New York tide. Danforth gave up singles to the first two batters he faced and Fohl, desperate for the victory, called on Shocker in relief despite the latter's complete game victory of the prior day. Shocker was simply not in condition to pitch so soon, and the Yankees came up with four runs. Fohl went with the now little-used Bill Bayne in the ninth and New York got another four runs – including Ruth's second home run of the game – and a final 11–6 victory.

The game was noteworthy from another standpoint. There have been previous references in this book to the dissension on the New York team. Perhaps one of the most graphic examples of this took place in the fifth inning. Robert Creamer in his *Babe: The Legend Comes to Life* recounts this incident:

> On July 26 in St. Louis Meusel and Schang tangled on the bench, and later Ruth and Pipp fought. Ruth had been riding Pipp about his fielding, which had fallen off slightly. In the last of the fifth Pipp bobbled a ball at first base. When he came in to the bench he said to Shawkey, "If that ape says one word, I'm going to belt him." Ruth trotted in from left field, came down the steps of the dugout and said: "For God's

sake, Pipp" and Pipp belted him. Wally was a big man, tall and rangy, and he had quick hands. He popped Ruth several times in the face with fast open-handed slaps as Ruth flailed wildly in return. They were pulled apart [Huggins, in the first base coaching box, called over plaintively, "Now stop that"], and Ruth said, "We'll settle this after the game."

"That's all right with me," Pipp said.

After the game, however, Ruth

came roaring and yelling into the clubhouse . . . and there was Pipp waiting for him. "I'm ready," Pipp said. Ruth looked at him in utter surprise, as if wondering what this was all about. Remembering, he waved his hand and said, "Oh, Christ, forget it."

The *New York Times* would comment:

Although Walter Pipp had something the better of Babe Ruth in a one-punch battle on the bench yesterday, truce has been declared. Ruth has calmed down a lot and Walter is strong in his calm indifference. He struck in self-defense it is said, and, according to Yank players, was fully justified in his action. Ruth is a bad matchmaker for himself, as Pipp is a clever and fearless fighter.

With the lead now down to a game and a half, Fohl called upon Vangilder to pitch the third game. And pitch he did, brilliantly, for seven innings as St. Louis carried a 2–1 lead into the eighth. Only Wally Pipp's fourth inning home run marred his performance. But the Yankees got to both him and Ray Kolp for four runs and a 5–2 margin going into the home ninth. The Browns, paced by Severeid's two-run double, tied up the game.

When Kolp allowed the first two Yankees to reach base in the tenth, Fohl waved Danforth in from the bullpen. The stage was now set for an incident which would affect the Browns' pennant chances and would not ultimately be resolved for almost an entire year. Danforth took over from Kolp after the latter had thrown two balls to pinch-hitter Elmer Smith. Huggins then countered by sending up Fred "Bootnose" Hofman, a righthanded hitter and St. Louis

Dave Danforth was sent to the minors in August 1922 for allegedly loading the seams of the ball in a game against the Yankees in July 1922. The following August he was again accused of doctoring the ball, but this time was the victor as Manager Lee Fohl was fired over the incident. (Photo courtesy of the *St. Louis Post-Dispatch.*)

native, who would ironically later serve as a coach for the Browns' 1944 pennant winners. After fouling off the first two pitches Hofman fanned on a shoulder-high fast ball.

"Take a look at that ball, Whitey [Witt, the next batter], it sailed a foot," said Hofman, as reported by the *Post-Dispatch*.

Witt asked plate umpire "Brick" Owens for an examination of the ball. Owens would later tell the newspaper:

> Whenever I find a pitcher has thrown a ball which has been tampered with it is my duty to expel that pitcher from the game. It matters not who doctored the ball. Anyone could easily perceive that mud had been rubbed into the seams on one side.
>
> After Hofman had fouled off two balls, I tossed out a new ball with which Danforth struck out the New York batter. I know the ball was new and clean when I delivered it to Catcher Severeid and when I next saw it I was convinced that it was what we term a "loaded ball."

Danforth appealed to the other umpire working the game, Tom Connolly, that he had done nothing more than rub some dust into the ball to take the new gloss off. This was a practice permitted under the rules. He would tell the *Post-Dispatch*: "I am willing to make a sworn statement that I did not in any illegal manner 'doctor' that ball. . . . If the ball was loaded then the loading was done by some other person and I was not aware that there was anything wrong with it when I pitched to Hofman."

Quinn wired Danforth's statement to American League President Ban Johnson, but to no avail. The customary ten-day suspension went into effect. Fohl, who according to Ray Gillespie never really believed Danforth, was particularly disturbed. The *Post-Dispatch* quoted him: "Dave has been warned often enough. It's hard on the club with Davis and Pruett out. Neither one of them will be able to work for four or five days."

Both Davis and Pruett had last worked in the Detroit game on July 23, but now Davis had an injured finger on his right hand and Pruett was nursing a sore arm. These injuries along with

Danforth's suspension forced Fohl to come back with Ray Kolp as a starter for the July 27 game. In the meantime Wayne Wright took over after Danforth's ejection and surrendered a home run to Wally Schang, which gave the Yankees a 6–5 win and reduced the Browns' lead to half a game.

In the finale Kolp lasted only two innings as New York got to him for four runs in the second with the highlight being Whitey Witt's three-run homer. Williams had given St. Louis hope in the first when he hit his twenty-third, but that was to be the bright spot of the game for the now second-place team. The final score was 7–3, with Bill Bayne pitching the final seven innings and giving up only two runs and four hits.

The Browns were now out of first place for the first time since June 16, and all St. Louis was in anguish. J. Roy Stockton reminded his readers that the three straight losses were a season high for the team while New York had at one time dropped eight in a row. Similarly, with the pitching problems what they were and with George Sisler's "slump" (he had dropped from .430 to .402 since July 7!), Stockton reassured that better things were in the offing.

Certainly such did not seem the case when Boston came in for a four-game series starting July 29. While Shocker worked his magic and scattered nine hits in the 4–1 triumph, both Sisler and Hank Severeid were injured. In the first inning Boston first baseman George Burns foul-tipped a ball which split the second finger on Severeid's right hand. The veteran catcher turned white, dropped off his mask, and staggered to the dugout in pain. Severeid was always fearful of someone taking over for him, but there was no choice in the matter. Pat Collins filled in and was to perform quite creditably in relief. But if Severeid's injury was not enough grief, more was to come.

In the fourth Sisler grounded to Burns, who was to be involved in both injuries, and each slid for the bag. While Sisler was called safe, it became apparent that Burns had spiked him in the mad dash for first. The Browns were now forced to shift Jacobson to first and move Shorten into center in addition to going with Collins behind the bat. The starting nine now had three players who were not regulars: Collins, Shorten, and Bronkie. The forecast on the time that both Sisler and Severeid would lose was ten days each, though Sisler felt he could play the next day. He couldn't, but miraculously, it didn't seem to matter.

The next day the patchwork lineup went out and beat Boston again by the same 4–1 count. Wright allowed only five hits, one a pinch-hit home run by Mike Menosky, while Williams hit number 26, and Tobin added one of his own. The result was a 6–2 victory and a game-and-a-half lead over the Yankees, who were losing to Chicago that day.

Late in the month it was announced that the Browns were considering adding some 7,000 temporary bleacher seats to bring the capacity of Sportsman's Park to 26,000. The move was designed to accommodate the hoped-for World Series crowds as well as the increased attendance expected from the tight pennant race. This news was also coupled with speculation that the team might spend as much as $200,000 on a permanent expansion.

6

AUGUST

Reinforcement from Boston

Ken Williams was now in the midst of the second of his three home run streaks of the season with number five in a row coming on August 1 as the Browns made it four in a row over the Red Sox 5–2. McManus also homered as Ray Kolp scattered eleven hits. The win extended the first place lead to two full games as the Yankees were rained out against Chicago.

The following day Philadelphia opened a four-game series with an 8–4 victory behind Eddie Rommel's pitching. Williams concluded his streak at six with number 28, but it was the only bright spot in the game for the Browns. Shocker was disturbingly ineffective, giving up three home runs, two doubles, one triple, and a single. Pruett relieved him and gave no reason for encouragement as he was nicked for two runs and six more hits.

Normality returned on August 3 as Bill Jacobson homered twice to account for five runs while Pat Collins connected for a three-run blast. Wright got the 9–5 victory, but needed help from Vangilder in the ninth. Herman Bronkie suffered at third, making three errors and hearing the wrath of the St. Louis fandom. Two of the errors figured in the Athletics' scoring. When the Browns took the field the next day the old pepper pot, Jimmy Austin, was at third. Frank Ellerbe was working out, but it was to be some time before his return.

Both clubs combined for 25 hits in the third game with St. Louis getting only 11. But they were the ones that counted as both John Tobin and Pat Collins homered while Tobin tripled twice. Despite being hit hard, Vangilder went the distance for the 9–4 win. The series closed on Saturday, August 5, with George Sisler returning to the lineup and responding with a single and a triple in the 4–1 triumph. Despite that and Pat Collins mimicking Ken Williams with his third home run in three days, the highlight of the game was a triple play by the Mackmen. And Sisler was the victim! Mack started Adolph Rettig (who, it will be recalled, stepped off the semi-pro sandlots to defeat the Browns back in July), and he walked the first two hitters, Gerber and Tobin. Rettig was quickly relieved by Eckert, who got two strikes on Sisler. On the next pitch he lined an apparent single to left and Gerber and Tobin both broke for the next base. However, Philadelphia shortstop "Chick" Galloway snared the ball and threw to second baseman "Pep" Young to get Gerber. Young relayed to Joe Hauser at first, and the Browns had experienced their third triple play of the season. (Mobile of the Southern Association and the Cleveland Indians had previously worked the play against the Browns.) Ray Kolp pitched another good effort for his tenth win of the season, scattering eight hits.

Washington came into Sportsman's Park after sweeping four in a row from the White Sox, but it mattered not to the Browns despite Walter Johnson's presence on the mound. The legendary "Big Train" surrendered only 97 home runs in his distinguished career, and John Tobin had two of these, one of which came on Sunday, August 6, with the bases filled. (Johnson allowed only one other bases-loaded homer among the 97.) Jim Tobin recalled this game:

> I know he hit two against Walter Johnson one time [actually the second was off Brillheart in the seventh inning] and I can tell you what Wally Johnson said to him.... "You

> little so and so, I didn't know where to throw them to you." . . . He was a pretty big man compared to John. I remember it because I happened to be on the bench when he came in there and he said, "You little so and so. I didn't know where to throw them." Well he used the regular [profane] language.

Fohl started Shocker, as was usually the case in series openers, and the veteran looked more in form than his last outing as he went the distance for the 8–4 victory. But all St. Louis was humming about hometown Tobin's two home runs. L. C. Davis wrote a special poem called "The Passing Show."

> When Johnny Tobin toed the pan
> He found the bases loaded
> Then to the joy of every fan
> A home run he exploded
> And then to emphasize the joke
> On Milan's pitching aces
> He gave the pill another poke
> That netted him four bases
>
> He is our favorite native son
> By overwhelming ballot
> For when the Browns need a run
> He swings a nasty mallet
> More power to his trusty stick
> For though it may seem funny
> He votes in the same bailiwick
> In which he draws his money

Tobin was St. Louis born and bred, first seeing the light of day on May 4, 1892. He had been a softball pitcher and corkball catcher before moving into baseball. He started as a pitcher for the Bell Telephone Company team, but it was his hitting that attracted attention, and Phil Ball signed him for his St. Louis Federal League team in 1913. After two years in the Federal League and one with Salt Lake City in the Pacific Coast League, Tobin was ready for the Browns. In 1917, playing the extended

Johnny Tobin during spring training at Mobile's Monroe Park. (Photo courtesy of Carita Jacobson Johnson.)

schedule common to the Pacific Coast League, the diminutive left-handed hitter had batted .331 in 187 games.

Sid Keener, writing in the *St. Louis Star Times*, recalled Tobin's "discovery" by Bob Quinn:

> I sat with Quinn in mid-season of 1917 and discussed the club's outlook for 1918. It was necessary to rebuild. Quinn

> sought outfield talent to aid Jacobson, then out in center field. Other fly chasers on the club did not impress Bob....
>
> Quinn told me of his long scouting expedition that carried him from the East to the Pacific coast.
>
> "I saw two boys who'll help us," said Quinn. "One is a St. Louis boy – a kid named Tobin, playing with Salt Lake City. To my surprise I found out he belongs to us on option. I've exercised the recall option. If ever a boy is ripe for the American League, Tobin is it."
>
> ...Tobin developed into the perfect ball player. He could drag bunt between the pitcher and first baseman, he could club them to right or left.... He could snatch down flies deep or in shallow right field, and he could throw with the accuracy of Enos Slaughter.... In his prime with the Brownies, Tobin bowed to no major league outfielder. He had one streak that is probably a record [no longer], although it isn't officially registered in the books. Anyway, Our Jawn [popular St. Louis nickname for Tobin] collected 200 or more hits for four straight seasons – 202 in 1920, 236 in 1921, 207 in 1922, and 202 in 1923. Ty Cobb, Tris Speaker, Babe Ruth, and Rogers Hornsby, four of the game's greatest swatters, failed to ever match that streak....

Tobin's greatest claim to fame as a player was his uncanny ability to drag bunt without any forewarning to opposing infielders. Observing the positioning of the second baseman, he could switch in a split second from a swinging stance to one in which he would be running as he slid his left hand up the bat with just the right touch to lay down the bunt.

As he later told Willis Johnson, who had returned to sportswriting with the old *St. Louis Globe*:

> With a player on first I hold my bat with both hands, and place the ball along the first base line, feeling confident that the man on first will reach second. With no one on base I loosen my hands entirely, allowing the bat to be free in the air just as the ball strikes the wood. I find it no trouble whatsoever to place the ball just between the reach of the pitcher and just short of the second baseman.

If August 6 was a great day for John Tobin, then August 7 was just as great for Ken Williams and the club as a whole. The Browns destroyed the Senators 16–1 as Williams homered twice in the sixth inning off starter George Mogridge and reliefer Eric Erickson. This established a new American League record, though the feat had been performed on five other occasions in the national and earlier major leagues. Both of the homers came with Jacobson on second base, each time as the result of a double. The Browns scored nine runs in the sixth inning while knocking out seven extra base hits, which established a new record for the major leagues that has been tied, but not surpassed to this date. Wayne Wright threw an eight-hitter and Pat Collins continued his home run heroics with one in the five-run eighth. Williams' two homers put him at 30 for the year.

Washington manager Clyde Milan sent future Brown Tom Zachary to the mound for the third game. Zachary would later gain dubious immortality when he would surrender Babe Ruth's sixtieth home run after returning to the Senators from the Browns early in the 1927 season. On this date, however, he was in excellent form as St. Louis could get only seven scattered hits and one run while Washington hit "Dixie" Davis in the pinches for eight hits and three runs. The lead over New York stood at one game.

The largely successful home stand came to an end on August 9 with an 8–6 win over the Senators. With the game tied 6–6 going into the seventh, the Browns got to Walter Johnson for the second time in four games by scoring two runs on a walk and two hits. Johnson had gone in to relieve the second Washington pitcher in the fourth. Vangilder was pounded out in the first inning, but Pruett eventually picked up the victory. McManus threw off a brief slump by homering in the third.

Despite the Browns having finished the home stand with an 11-5 record, *Post-Dispatch* writer Dent McSkimming was cautious as the team prepared for their final road trip of the season:

In that interval [three weeks] they will meet every other club in the league starting with Chicago on Saturday. The Yankees meanwhile, will be at the Polo Grounds. In view of the fact that both the New York and St. Louis clubs have established themselves as better "home" clubs than "road" clubs, it becomes evident that St. Louis for the moment faces the most unpromising outlook of the two contenders.

Club officials, Manager Fohl and his players are a unit in regarding the forthcoming trip as the decisive test of St. Louis strength. The fact that the Browns have just completed a home stand which may be regarded as highly successful would seem to indicate that the club is in a winning mood and may make a better showing on the road than heretofore.

McSkimming quoted Fohl's feelings as the trip began:

Of course, I am making no predictions. But if we don't win a large percentage of our 24 games on this trip it will not be because of adverse circumstances before the journey. Conditions indicate that we should enjoy the best journey of the year.

We have not had a really good trip yet. The club has had no real winning streak (on the road). Except for the absence of Severeid and Ellerbe–and both men will probably be in the game soon–the club is well fixed for the trip.

When George Sisler returned to the lineup Fohl moved Jacobson to left field and Williams to center rather than returning "Jake" to his familiar spot. Fohl explained his reasons to McSkimming:

I expect the team to profit greatly through the shift in outfielders which puts Williams in center and Jacobson in left. Williams covers a remarkable amount of territory, he has become a sure fielder of ground balls and his arm is superior to Jacobson's. Williams should cut off a lot of extra bases on hits. His margin of superiority in fielding should result in holding the opposing team to two or three bases less per game than would Jake.

> Jacobson, I feel equally sure, will find left field to his taste. He will be required to cover less ground than he did in center and the position should be relatively easy for him.

The series at Chicago was only two games, and the first marked the return of Severeid behind the plate, though the middle finger of his throwing hand was far from healed. Shocker pitched for the Browns and stayed until the ninth inning despite being knocked for seventeen hits. McSkimming described his efforts as "the lax hurling of the once great spitball pitcher," as if it could be expected that Shocker would be no longer effective in the future. St. Louis led 7–2 going into the ninth, but Chicago rallied with four runs. Pruett and Wright combined to hold the victory. George Sisler collected three hits and moved ahead of Ty Cobb in the American League batting race with a .412 mark against .409 for Cobb.

On August 13 Severeid got his first hit since returning, but it mattered for little as Chicago got to Vangilder in the second inning for six hits and ultimately scored six runs in the 9–3 rout.

Severeid was the oldest regular on the club, having joined the team for the 1915 season. In his first game he hit a grand slam homer off Chicago White Sox pitcher Hi Jasper, who had given up only one other hit, to win the game 4–3. Born in Story City, Iowa, on June 1, 1891, the workhorse catcher moved from semi-pro ball to Cincinnati in July 1910. Over the next two and a half years he played in 80 games for the Reds, but asked to be sent to the minors so that he could play daily. After an outstanding year at Louisville he and another player were sold to the Browns for $30,000 in late 1914. Over the next three seasons Severeid developed into the Browns' regular catcher and had the distinction of catching two successive no-hit games. This historic event, which has never been equaled, occurred when Bob Groom and Erie Koob pitched the Browns to victory over the league champion White Sox, 3–0 and 1–0, on May 5–6, 1917.

After World War I service in France Severeid returned to the

Browns and began the most productive period of his career with batting marks of .324 in 1921, .321 in 1922, .309 in 1923, and .308 in 1924. Always the cagey veteran, sometimes after a young player would draw a walk, he would hold the ball and kick the dirt, as if disgusted with the umpire. Then he would whirl and throw to first, timing the throw so the ball would reach the first baseman an instant after the runner reached the bag. Frequently he'd get a pick-off since many players would step off the bag after being awarded a base on balls!

The Browns brought with them on this road trip their young mascot, Joey Ryan of Terra Haute, Indiana. McSkimming commented: "The appearance of little Joey Ryan, the 12-year-old Brownie mascot, was greeted with generous applause. The youngster was bedecked in a new traveling uniform and made a most favorable impression. Manager Kid Gleason of the Sox was much taken with him and gave him an opportunity to show off for the fans in fielding."

Both Dorothy Tobin Brady and her uncle Jim had recollections of Ryan. Dorothy Brady:

> He [John Tobin] was crazy about that kid. My father was very fond of children. Extremely fond of children. And he had him [Ryan] at our house many times and . . . a few of the other players got together or my dad did this, but I know he was in on this. They dress him [Ryan] all up, they brought him nice slacks and like the vaudeville people used to wear years ago. . . . The men would wear the striped blazers, the straw kaddie hats, and the little cane, and they would teach him to do the cakewalk. . . . He was quite a strutter. And . . . I think he would have gone over in vaudeville very well. And [he had] a lot of personality and the ball players just got a great big kick out of him and really liked him and I think did an awful lot of things for him.

Jim Tobin:

> He'd come out and catch on first base once in awhile. . . . I guess everybody took a liking to him and he'd get out on

> the field and show off at first base. . . . He was around quite a bit and then I think he did go away with them [Browns] on some of the trips . . . I don't think he was [there for more than the 1922 season].

As the Browns trained east from Chicago on their final road trip, McSkimming mused over the pitching performances of the last three days. Vangilder had been pounded very hard in two of the games and Shocker was unimpressive in the other. Still the team had won two of the three games, resorting to the heavy hitting that always seemed to bail them out. The staff would face a particularly tough test in Washington with a five-game set (including two doubleheaders) facing them due to previous washouts.

While the team enjoyed two days on the train some interesting developments were occurring with respect to Danforth and Shorten. It will be recalled that Danforth had been suspended following the game in late July against the Yankees when he was ejected for allegedly loading the seams of the ball. The Browns were able to waive Danforth through the American League and sent him to their Tulsa farm club of the Western League. Danforth protested vigorously (see Appendix B), but agreed to report. He played no further role in 1922, but the matter would not be ultimately resolved until 1923.

On August 14 "Chick" Shorten participated in what must be regarded as an early forerunner to the present-day All-Star game (which did not formally begin until 1933). On that date in Boston a team of American League All-Stars defeated the Boston Red Sox 3–2. The game was played for the benefit of the family of former Red Sox player Tom McCarthy, who had passed away earlier in the month. Some 4,000 attended and raised about $5,000 for the McCarthy family.

Shorten represented the Browns and went zero for four. Other teams contributed the balance of the lineup: Philadelphia was represented by "Pep" Young, "Doc" Johnston, "Tillie" Walker, Frank Bruggy, and Bob Hasty; Elmer Smith and "Bootnose"

Hoffman played for New York; Ira Flagstead came from Detroit; Donnie Bush and Nick Altrock represented Washington; Hervey McClelland came from Chicago; and Cleveland sent Jim Bagby and Les Nunamaker. In an interesting precedent, "Lizzie" Murphy, a woman player with the Providence All-Stars, played first base for the American League team for one inning. She grounded out in her one plate appearance. The All-Stars won the game in the tenth when Johnston tripled home Young.

The Browns were due into Washington at 6 p.m. on August 14, and shortly thereafter someone else would be due in to join them. The third base problem had continued to plague the club: Ellerbe's knee was slow to come around; Bronkie could hit well enough, but was slow on the base paths and unreliable in the field. Austin, who was now filling in, was at an advanced age, and he too had just come up injured. Quinn had earlier tried to obtain Eddie Foster from Boston, but was unable to get him via the waiver route. Now that route opened up and the Browns, rather than New York, got help from Boston.

Foster had been used by the Red Sox in a utility role, though at one time he had been a stellar third baseman. From 1912 to 1919 the now 34-year-old player had been Washington's hot corner man. Clark Griffith, Washington owner, had named him to his all-Senator's team, and he was known equally for his fighting spirit, his place-hitting ability, and his clever fielding. Griffith regarded Foster as second only to Willie Keeler as a place-hitter, while Walter Johnson attributed much of his success to Foster's fielding. When Johnson's speed encouraged rivals to bunt, Foster developed as one of the cleverest fielders of bunts, his one-hand, one-motion scoops to first base setting the style for that kind of play.

Frank Ellerbe roomed with Foster at Washington in 1919 and recalled an amusing incident:

> Eddie came to us. He and I were good friends on the Washington ball club. . . . He and I were rooming together. It would get hot as the devil there in St. Louis, Chicago and

> those places in the summertime. Nights were just as hot as the daytime, the hot air coming off those wheat fields out there in the West. Anyway, why Eddie was just stripped naked and turned the bathtub full of water as cool as he could get it. He jumped in the bathtub and jumped back in bed. I said: "Eddie, you're going to wet that bed all over." "Yeah, Gov, it'll dry off too quick (to matter)!" . . . Two or three (times) a night some times, he'd jump in that tub and then jump back in bed.

The *Post-Dispatch*'s L. C. Davis took Foster's acquisition as an occasion to write one of his poems, appropriately entitled "Eddie Foster":

> The Brownies determined to capture the flag
> Have added a guy to their roster
> To plug up the hole at the difficult bag
> None other than old Eddie Foster
> Although he may not be a Frisch or a Groh
> He's clever and steady as infielders go
>
> The Brownies went into the enemies camp
> And got him on waivers from Boston
> And few are possessed of three men of the stamp
> Of Ellerbe, Foster and Austin
> Though one is a cripple and one is passe
> Of infielding talent they're quite an array
>
> In lieu of a national bank or a mine
> The Brownies secured him by waivers
> And thousands of customers freely opine
> That Eddie will be a life saver
> The purchase involving no bundle of swag
> They cannot accuse us of buying the flag

The opening game of the doubleheader with Washington on August 15 certainly gave McSkimming no cause to change his feelings about the Browns' pitching. Wright started and left after the sixth trailing 3–0. Pruett relieved, but could do no better as the Senators won 6–1. Bronkie played third for Austin as Foster had not yet arrived and did so again in the second game. "Dixie" Davis pitched nine excellent innings in this game as the Browns collected 12 hits off Washington pitcher Ray Francis for the 7–1 win.

Pruett's poor performance in the first game increased speculation that he might be lost for the season because of a sore arm. In late July Fohl had given Pruett a two-week rest and indicated that the rookie would be used only for relief work for the balance of the season. However, recent relief appearances had shown that his "screwball" or "fadeaway" did not break and he relied mainly on his curve and fastball. With his pitching inventory thus reduced the University of Missouri grad was much less effective. If Pruett were out of the picture it would leave the club with only one lefthander, Bill Bayne. Fortunately such was not to be the case.

Foster joined in time to play both ends of the August 16 doubleheader and went two for five in the first game, a 7–3 victory. Shocker went the distance and seemed to show no effects from a batting practice accident of the previous day. (Fielding at third, he had been caught in the left thigh with a line drive from Bronkie's bat.) He shook off the sting, but observers at the time thought there was room for concern. Fohl took Foster's arrival as an opportunity to shake up the batting order by returning Tobin to lead-off and batting Foster second to take advantage of his hit and run talents.

The second game saw Ray Kolp lose his effectiveness and depart in the second inning. Bayne relieved him, but after three innings Washington led 7–0 and eventually won 11–3. The game was marked by the appearance of three little-used players: pitcher Henry Meine, who pitched the last four innings; third baseman Gene Robertson, who got two hits off Walter Johnson; and catcher Josh Billings, who got one of his three hits of the season in this game. The contest was also marked by some classic delaying tactics by Ken Williams, who hoped to get the game cancelled when rain threatened. The *Post-Dispatch*'s Dent McSkimming relates the incident:

> In the last half of the fourth inning, Harris hit a bounder over second base. Two were out. Williams fielded the ball and held it while Harris continued to second. Harris invited Williams to make a play at second retiring the side and thus hastening the game. Washington was leading 7 runs to 2. Williams, however, declined to put Harris out and the Washington man continued to third.
>
> Still Williams held the ball, declining to make an attempt to catch Harris. Harris continued for home and beat Williams' throw to the plate by five feet.
>
> Umpire Connolly did not admonish Williams at the time, but he later declared his intention to make a written report of the incident.

The split, though unsatisfying, did give the Browns a full-game lead over the Yankees, who were beaten by Detroit. The series concluded the next day when St. Louis waited until the ninth inning before teeing off on George Mogridge and reliever Ray Francis for eight runs. Washington got three more themselves in the home half of the ninth, but the final read 8–5. Davis once again looked sharp and only yielded in the ninth to Wright when Washington rallied.

Back home in St. Louis, the Missouri Theater announced that the week of August 19 would be Browns Week. Moviegoers would be treated to the first complete motion pictures of the team in action in addition to the theater's normal fare. In the theater's ad for the promotion a telegram from Washington, D.C., dated August 14, was reproduced:

> Manager Goldman
> Missouri Theater, St. Louis
>
> Every member of the St. Louis Browns wishes to congratulate the management of the Missouri Theater for staging a Browns' Booster Week, from Manager Lee Fohl down to little Joe Ryan, the mascot. All were exceedingly glad to hear that they were being thought of in such a novel manner before the eyes of the St. Louis fans on the screen of the beautiful Missouri Theater. Boys, what could be sweeter! A

> word of encouragement just now to the Fighting Browns means a great deal, especially when it comes from the home-town folks. Here's hoping BROWNS' WEEK at the MISSOURI THEATER proves a huge success, a regular World Series.
>
> WILLIS E. JOHNSON
> Traveling Secretary

The Browns moved on to Philadelphia for single games on August 18 and 20 with a doubleheader on the 19th. The series would see them lose the league lead briefly and hardly make them seem like a team to be viewed with awe at the Missouri Theater. In the opener, St. Louis caught the Athletics coming off a three-game winning streak which they proceeded to extend to four at the expense of the Browns. Vangilder's slump continued, and he failed to get past the second inning. Jacobson celebrated his return to center field with a home run, but it was all there was to celebrate in the 8–4 defeat.

The hitters came back in the first game of the doubleheader to provide Shocker with enough support to gain a 9–5 win. Shocker was pressed in the early going, but his spitter worked well in the later stages. Williams got his thirty-first home run in this game and his thirty-second in the second, a 6–5 loss. It was a costly defeat as the Yankees moved into first place by a half-game through their victory over Chicago. "Rasty" Wright carried a 5–4 lead into the seventh when his control failed him. With a runner on first Wright's knuckleball delivery to Joe Hauser went for a wild pitch, advancing the runner to third. Hauser then tripled and the game was tied. Then in the eighth "Bing" Miller put a Wright pitch into the seats and the Browns were in second place. McSkimming felt that Fohl probably should have pulled Wright earlier: "If Manager Fohl's pitchers were all going well, especially had Pruett been strong and ready, it is probable that Wright would have been withdrawn at this point. But, with pitchers worrying along as best they may, Wright was made to remain."

Foster continued his strong play since joining the team, going five for seven over the course of the doubleheader. The hits were collected in consecutive times at bat. McManus had a home run in the second game.

It was more gloom on the 20th as Davis' successful pitching stretch came to an end. He failed to get a man out and gave up a home run to Frank Welch before Fohl pulled him. Kolp relieved, but Philadelphia catcher Cy Perkins got a home run from him to make it 5–0. The Browns came back to make it close, but the Athletics took it 7–6. With the Yankees idle, St. Louis now fell a full game out of first place. L. C. Davis reflected the despair:

> The Brownies now tied in the race*
>   for the wreath
>   Are not feeling gay and hilarious
> While still hanging on by the skin
>   of their teeth
>   Their tenure is very precarious
> Though recently adding some
>   strength to their ranks**
> They're having their trouble in
>   shaking the Yanks

But if the Browns despaired after losing three of four to Philadelphia, it took only a three-game sweep in Boston and the recapture of first place to restore confidence before the big four-game series in New York. Shocker looked his old self on August 21, giving the Red Sox only seven hits in the 9–4 triumph. On the following day the Browns slipped back into first by a half-game with their 6–3 victory while Cleveland was defeating the Yankees. Fohl started Wright, but despite a 4–1 lead pulled him when the first two batters in the fourth doubled and singled. Vangilder came in to relieve and looked like the Vangilder of old. Over the last three innings he gave up only three hits. Williams and Sisler went wild on the base paths as each stole two bases on

**Not quite; they were one game behind.*
***Foster.*

Boston catcher "Muddy" Ruel. (Ruel would later manage the 1947 Browns.)

August 24 saw the Browns come up with one of those games not untypical for a team with six .300 hitters in the lineup. Raking three Boston pitchers for twenty hits, they coasted to a 13–2 win, scoring nine runs in the first two innings. Ray Kolp allowed the Red Sox only six hits, and Fohl once again went to the bench, relieving Foster with Robertson and Severeid with Billings. The latter got the final two hits of his 1922 career and also managed to commit an error. Williams extended his hitting streak to 28 games and would see it end there.

Speculation was now rampant as to Fohl's pitching plans for the series with the Yankees. The normal procedure would have seen Shocker pitch the first game of the doubleheader, scheduled for Friday, August 25, and perhaps come back for the final game on Sunday. But now "Dixie" Davis' recent strong performances gave rise to the idea of letting him go the "ironman" route. Assuming a strong performance in the first game, Davis would then pitch the second. Severeid urged this approach, which Fohl pondered long and hard.

Back in St. Louis the formation of a Pennant Boosters Club was announced. At a meeting of civic organizations at the Hotel Statler it was agreed to form an organization to aid the two St. Louis teams in their quest for the respective pennants of the American and National leagues. St. Louis Mayor Henry Kiel was named honorary chairman as the group drew up the following creed:

> In becoming a member of the St. Louis Pennant Boosters Club I pledge myself at all times to be a loyal St. Louisian.
>
> To encourage by every fair means the success of our baseball teams.
>
> To withhold criticism of all kinds and be a constant booster, believing that success comes from positive rather than negative action.
>
> To discourage remarks that though perhaps well meant, affect the morale of the team.

> I agree to attend every game I possibly can between now and the end of the season and to aid by my moral support the bringing of the pennants to St. Louis and also the world's championship.
>
> This I subscribe to as a 100 per cent red blooded St. Louis fan.

While the Cardinals were at the time in second place, the National League race was in no way as intense as that of the American. Pennant fever was sweeping St. Louis, but it was Browns fever. Accordingly those involved with the new group thought it would be appropriate to stage a civic reception and dinner for the Browns on their return from the current road trip. Fohl was fearful—with just cause—that such events were quite premature and could do the team no good. He wired Quinn his concern:

> I have been informed through telegrams and through stories that appear in the Eastern papers that our good friends back home, in an admirable display of enthusiasm and desire to reward the Browns for their splendid fight, have laid plans for some sort of reception when the club arrives at home.
>
> I regret very much that I must cast water on such a flame now that it has been many years since St. Louis baseball fans have been moved to such a pitch of excitement.
>
> But, neither I nor my players believe that it would be a good thing for the team if they were feted and dined and entertained before the pennant fight is completed.
>
> We are very happy to know that so many business men and men in public office and civic organizations and a great host of baseball enthusiasts have taken hold of the idea to show their appreciation to the players. We know, too, that they desire to please us by any demonstration they may indulge in. Therefore I wish that you would express to them our desire that they alter their plans.
>
> One reason that we object is because we know that it would hurt rather than aid the morale of the club. Another reason is that there remains a possibility that we will finish behind the Yankees.

> If we should fail to win the pennant after being proclaimed champions we would become the butt of endless jokes and slurs the seasons to come.

Fohl was also echoing the feelings of the players, and the message got through. There was no reception. Nor would there be.

Originally a three-game set, the final Polo Grounds games with the Yankees became a four-game affair when one of the July games was rained out. Fohl discarded the idea of a "Dixie" Davis "ironman" attempt and went with Shocker in the first game of the doubleheader. Normally regarded as a Yankee killer, the staff ace had only a 3–5 record against his former team. Some 38,000 fans were on hand for the two games despite threatening weather. The *New York Times* described the scene:

> Every vehicle, of whatever order, subway, elevated and surface cars, automobiles, express wagons, anything that was expected or could be bribed to make its way to the ball park was jammed to the guards or the gunwale from noon onward and near riots among the surging populace, both at transportation points and outside the Polo Grounds, were common. It was just about the most determined and intent outpouring ever seen for games in a pennant chase. Nearly half an hour before the opening game began the sale of grandstand seats was stopped and late comers either were shooed into the bleachers or wended their way homeward.
>
> Inside the park the scene was stirring long before there was anything stirring on the greensward below. Every seat in the grandstand was occupied and rows of standees in the rear encircled the structure. By the time that the initial tussle was under way the bleachers were comfortably filled and later arrivals filled these outfield seats so thoroughly that only by raising the center field screens could more people have been accommodated.

The Browns struck in the second inning for an early 1–0 lead, which would have proved enough to win the game as Shocker responded with one of his classic efforts. Jacobson singled to right and went to second on McManus' ground-out. Hank Severeid then sent one of Yankee starter Waite Hoyt's deliveries to deep center. Jacobson easily scored and Severeid, no speed demon, charged into third with a triple.

In the sixth Foster and Sisler led off with singles. Williams flied to "Whitey" Witt in center with Foster advancing to third after the catch. Jacobson then walked to load the bases. This brought up McManus, who took Hoyt's first pitch and drilled it to left, scoring Foster and Sisler. Carrying a 3–0 lead into the bottom of the ninth Shocker faltered, but only momentarily. Dugan and Ruth led off with singles, but then Shocker got Pipp to foul out to Foster and struck out Wally Schang. Bob Meusel then singled in Dugan for the Yankees' lone run. Shocker got the third out when Ward popped out to Foster. The Browns now had a game-and-a-half lead and would never be in better shape.

Ken Williams' failure to connect brought his hitting streak to an end at 28 games. At this point it was the longest hitting streak of the season. George Sisler had then hit in 24 straight games and would go far beyond that. Williams' hometown of Grant's Pass, Oregon, was so pleased by the overall great season he was enjoying that they passed a resolution of appreciation and forwarded a copy to the Browns slugger.

Davis started game two for Fohl and hardly gave evidence of any "ironman" potential. After walking Witt and hitting Dugan, he gave up a triple to Ruth, giving New York a quick 2–0 lead. After he threw two balls to Wally Pipp, Fohl yanked him and went to Vangilder. The latter got out of the inning after allowing the Yankees one more run. But the Browns refused to roll over and play dead. In the third, "Bullet" Joe Bush, the New York starter, fed a home run ball to Wally Gerber for his first and only four-bagger of the season. The Yankees got that one back in their half of the inning and picked up two more in the fourth. In this inning Pruett made one of his now infrequent appearances. He fanned Ruth, which had come to be expected, and then retired Pipp on a liner to Sisler. But then Schang singled to score two previous runners that Vangilder had put on to make it 6–1.

Pruett's condition continued to perplex both his teammates and himself. The *Post-Dispatch* talked to both Wayne Wright and Elam Vangilder. Wright said:

> It is my opinion that Pruett has not permanently hurt any ligament in his arm. From what he tells me of the arm I believe that he has contracted a cold in the elbow very much the same as I did a couple of years ago. Warm weather, hot weather, and rest should put him back in shape within a month.

Vangilder:

> A bad shoulder is the real serious proposition. About three years ago I tore a muscle partly loose in my right shoulder and the Tulsa club gave me the gate. They thought sure I was finished as a pitcher. . . . A mere strain in the elbow is comparatively a minor injury.

Pruett himself downplayed the possibility that he had perhaps injured the arm through early season overwork. He pointed out that at Tulsa the prior season he had on occasion worked seven games a week without ill effect. He similarly dismissed those who believed his use of the "screwball" might be the problem, and stated:

> I notice an immediate improvement after a little rest. Probably if I had been able to rest from the time I first hurt the arm until now I would be ready to pitch every fourth day. It was not Manager Fohl's fault that I did not rest. He wanted me to take all the time I needed, but I was anxious to get back in the box and pitch.

Fohl let Pruett complete the fourth and fifth innings and then went with Bill Bayne the rest of the way. St. Louis picked up a single run in the fifth and another in the seventh when Johnny Tobin hit a solo homer. Going into the ninth New York had a comfortable 6–3 lead until Bush tired. Shorten, batting for Bayne, singled, and Tobin followed with a triple. Huggins brought in "Sad Sam" Jones, and he retired Foster and Sisler, but Tobin scored on the latter's ground-out. But it was not over yet. Williams singled and Jacobson walked to increase the tension. McManus came up with visions, no doubt, of duplicating his first-game heroics. Such was not the case as Jones bore down and got McManus to fly out to end the game.

New York baseball writer Davis Walsh, writing in the *Post-Dispatch*, would later overdramatize this particular game, claiming that a hit here (by McManus) could have won the pennant for the Browns. As we have seen and will see, the same could be said for any number of games.

Saturday, August 26, dawned gray and overcast over New York, and the weather would be reflected in both the attendance and the Browns' performance. Only 12,000 came out as rain fell at intervals throughout the game. Wayne "Rasty" Wright was the Browns' starter, while Huggins selected Carl Mays, with whom St. Louis had had reasonable success earlier in the season. Today they would have no success with him as he would scatter ten hits en route to a 9–2 win and the league lead by half a game. Wright lasted six innings, principally because he gave the Yankees their runs in two- and one-run increments rather than in clusters. When he batted in the fifth inning the occasion prompted this observation of Lee Fohl by the *New York Times* writer covering the game:

> The first words spoken by Lee Fohl, as far as can be discovered, since his arrival in this fair city were uttered from the third base coaching line in the fifth inning and were audible as far as third base. Umpire Evans called Wright's thrust down the line past Fohl foul and Lee thought it was fair. He made weird, disapproving motions with his lips, but nobody could make out what his argument was.

The rain which threatened to postpone Saturday's game succeeded in postponing the Sunday contest to Monday's open date. Despite the weather some 15,000 fans showed up at the Polo

Grounds hoping to see the game get underway. Yankee officials waited more than half an hour past the normal starting time before calling it off. And wait they might, as the cancellation gave Shocker another day of rest and allowed him to start the Monday game. While the Yankees had had good success against Shocker this season, they of course would have desired to avoid him.

With an off day to ponder in depth the Browns' pennant hopes, *Post-Dispatch* writer Dent McSkimming calculated that the team would have to win 22 of its remaining 30 games to finish first. He was not far off; if that had in fact occurred St. Louis would have finished with a 95-59 record, one game better than the Yankees' actual 94-60 mark. But that was September talk. The immediate problem was to bring the team back to first place.

Once again the day was dark and chilly, holding the attendance down to about 20,000. Miller Huggins selected another of his aces, Bob Shawkey, to start. The old cliche "classic pitching duel" is the most accurate description of the game. Shawkey would give the Browns only four hits while the Yankees got double that, but the game would nonetheless be decided in extra innings by one run. New York scored first in the second inning when, with one out, Schang singled to center. After Meusel flied to Jacobson light-hitting Aaron Ward, the Yankee second baseman tripled into left center for a 1–0 lead.

The Browns got that one back when Hank Severeid homered into the left field bleachers. *The New York Times* reported that "Severeid jogged around the highways to the music of rousing cheers by little Joe Ryan, the Browns' mascot, who permitted Hank to shake his hand after crossing the plate." The *New York Daily News'* James Cruisinberry observed that "Severeid's four baser knocked some one cuckoo in the bleachers and a doctor was summoned to give aid." It would be the only damage that the Browns would do to anyone that day.

The game continued tied. In the eighth, with Tobin on first and two out, Sisler singled to right as Tobin headed to third. With his great speed Sisler gambled that he could make second, allowing the go ahead run to score. He lost the gamble as Ruth's throw to

Scott got him at second. In the Yankee ninth Pipp sent Tobin back to the wall with a fly that, had it been a foot higher, would have ended the game. But the Browns had one more memorable threat. In the tenth, with two out and Gerber on second via a single and Tobin at first on a walk, Shawkey faltered. The *New York Daily News'* James Cruisinberry reported:

> Eddie Foster was at bat and he connected for a fierce drive ten feet over third base. The ball crashed against the left wall on first bound and Gerber dashed home and Tobin went all the way to third as Bob Meusel winged the ball to that corner. Then it was discovered that Umpire Moriarty had declared the drive foul. Boss Fohl of the Browns, who was coaching at third, raised Ned about it, claiming it was fair. But the ump's verdict stood. Foster returned to the plate, the boys went back to first and second and were left there when Foster popped up an easy foul. It was a close call and possibly the pennant depended on it.

George Sisler, years later during spring training in Florida, would recall the incident. As he told Tom Meany for the latter's *Baseball's Greatest Teams*: "I can still see in my mind where the ball hit. It was a fair ball."

In the eleventh Dugan opened with a single off Shocker. After Ruth went out, Pipp sent a long single to right, sending Dugan to third. Fohl had Shocker pass Schang to load the bases to set up the hoped-for, inning-ending double play. The Yankees went a game and a half up when Meusel flied deep enough to Tobin to allow Dugan to score the winning run.

Despite the Browns' losing the series three games to one and falling into second, events would prove that the pennant race was far from over. Nonetheless L. C. Davis seemed to be conceding to the Yankees:

> We thought we had a winning team
> But New York banished all our hope
> Which proves the check book is supreme
> In spite of all contrary dope

Although we're trailing in the race
Our heroes gave the best they had
We're fighting now for second place
Which after all is not so bad.

While Davis may have been writing off the Browns, Miller Huggins was not. The Yankees might be in first place, but Huggins conceded that the pennant fight would be tough, though he expected to win it. His caution was perhaps influenced by the state of the Cleveland pitching staff. The Browns opened a three-game series with the Indians on August 29 and would not have to face either of Cleveland's top pitchers. Both Stan Coveleski and Guy Morton had been sidelined (by intestinal problems and tonsilitis, respectively). The nature of their illnesses was such as to insure that they would not be ready for September 4–6, a four-game series at St. Louis. On the other hand it was apparent that both would return to the rotation in time to face the Yankees in Cleveland September 22–24.

For most of the first game of the Cleveland series it hardly mattered that neither ace pitcher was available or that playing manager Tris Speaker was also out with a bad knee. Georg Uhle, the Cleveland pitcher, one-hit the Browns until two were out in the eighth. With the Indians ahead 2–1 Uhle blew up by walking two, hitting one, and giving up four hits which produced five runs and a 6–3 Browns victory. St. Louis won the game on only five hits while Cleveland got nine. Kolp picked up the win, but needed help from Vangilder.

The second game was also close with the Browns holding only a 5–3 lead going into the ninth. This time it was "Duster" Mails' turn to blow up as the Browns hammered him for seven hits which produced six runs. Vangilder, who was now being used extensively in relief, took over from starter Wayne Wright when the Indians put two men on in the bottom of the ninth.

But the Browns were not to have it their way for all of this series. Cleveland pulled their own late-inning comeback in the August 31 game. With "Dixie" Davis holding a comfortable 6–2 lead, the Indians proceeded to collect five runs on a walk, wild throw, and five hits. Vangilder relieved again, but this time could do no good and was tagged with the 7–6 loss.

As August closed the Browns were now two full games behind New York. They had been in the lead at the end of both June and July.

7

SEPTEMBER

"I Benched Davis . . . to Get Rid of Smith"

When the Browns arrived in Detroit for their final away games of the season, they arrived without Joe Ryan, who had returned to Terre Haute for the opening of the school year. They did bring along Urban Shocker, who pitched one of his standard openers, defeating the Tigers 4–1. The second game, on September 2, was particularly significant for a number of reasons: the 5–4 win brought the Browns back to within one and a half games of first, George Sisler hit in his 30th consecutive game, and "Hub" Pruett showed his best form since early July. Pitching in relief of Kolp, the rookie lefthander gave up only three hits in four innings to earn the victory. With the score tied 4–4 in the eighth, the winning run came in when McManus flied out with Foster scoring. Pruett showed no pain and worked easily. Jim Tobin remembered Pruett's pitching and shed some light on his problem: "He threw too much with his arm a lot of times. He didn't have that follow through all the time. . . . You like to get a sore arm in a hurry [that way], but he was good."

The Browns could pick up no further ground and in fact dropped back to two games off the pace when they failed to score on another "Eddie Foster incident." As in the game against the Yankees the previous Monday, Foster came up with men on base in extra innings. This time it was the eleventh and the bases were filled. Foster again poked a ball down the left field line, which Detroit left fielder Bobby Veach caught with his bare hand. The Tigers got the winning run in the last of the eleventh for the 4–3 victory.

The team returned home to open their final stand of the season with a morning-afternoon doubleheader against Cleveland. The *Post-Dispatch*'s Dent McSkimming concluded that the Browns would have to win 19 of their remaining 23 games to win the American League, but that they were in an excellent position to do so:

> The Browns are a .704 club on their home grounds. There is no reason to believe they will strike a slump in this final stay. They should travel closer to .800 because of the impetus to be gathered in the pennant drive. . . .
>
> The Browns are the most popular ball club in the American League. The Yankees, meanwhile, will find every other one of the seven opposing teams a bitter antagonist. The Yanks will have to be a much better ball club than the Browns to win the same number of games from now to the end. . . .
>
> When the Browns recently played a series in New York the cheering of the fans was almost equally divided. There did not appear to be whole-hearted support of the New York Americans, even among the home town fans. Ruth and Dugan were jeered at times, just as they were at St. Louis. Sisler, Williams, Tobin and others of the Brownies received an encouraging round of applause on almost every trip to the plate. At Chicago, Cleveland, Philadelphia and Boston it would appear from the cheering of the fans, that the Browns were the home club. . . .
>
> During the long stand at Sportsman's Park which opened today, the fans are sure to see an improved Urban Shocker, a greatly improved Kenney Williams and a wonderful little ball player at third base in Eddie Foster.

McSkimming then went to a quick rundown of the pitching staff:

> Shocker was never better, which is to say is the equal of any pitcher in the league.
> Davis is erratic, but in excellent form and capable of pitching a wonderful game.
> Wright . . . has in his repertoire a knuckleball which fools the catcher, but has never reached the maxium effectiveness, because he has not mastered control. When he does he can take his place beside Shocker.
> Vangilder, the hard luck pitcher of the season, was one of the league's leading hurlers at the start of the season and is expected to grow constantly better as the cool weather comes on.
> Kolp should be most valuable as a relief hurler.
> Pruett, just recovered from a sore arm, would be one of the game's greatest pitchers could he develop a fast ball. From now to the end of the race he should prove invaluable as a relief pitcher.
> Bayne may at any moment turn out to be a grand pitcher. He was all of that last year and has given every indication recently of returning to his best form.

Quinn, who was with the club in Cleveland conferring with Indians officials on how to run a World Series (Cleveland won it in 1920), had his hands full with crowd problems on Labor Day. The morning game was scheduled to begin at 10:30, but the late arrival of the Cleveland club delayed its start until about 11:20. The crowd was kept out of the park for a time as it was felt the game might not be played. When that possibility did not occur the entry of the crowd caused the game to be further delayed. All but the last few thousand were coming in as play got underway.

But that was a small problem compared to what would happen after the first game. That contest ended about 1:00 p.m. and many of those present wanted to remain in their seats for the second game. However, in this era admission was charged for both ends of a doubleheader, and the park was eventually cleared. It was estimated that as many as ten thousand people were milling outside the field by the time the gates were opened for the afternoon game scheduled to start at 3:00 p.m. The crowd was so dense and formed so early that the police could do little to control them. Gates were pushed in and fence boards removed; many were able to enter without paying.

As was customary in those days, overflow crowds were allowed on the field, held back by ropes. Fans who had been happy with the seats in the temporary bleachers were not so pleased when the second wave of patrons, six deep on the field, formed in front of them. All told about 25,000 attended the afternoon game while 15,000 were on hand for the morning affair.

L. C. Davis thought the occasion merited a poem, which he called "Hot Stuff":

A diller, a dollar
A 10:30 scholar
What makes you come so late?
It peeves the fans
Upsets their plans
And makes them crash the gate

It's always hot weather
When fans get together
And storm the baseball lot
They made a big holler
And under the color
They all got very hot

But when they were seated
And royally treated
Their woes they soon forgot
The frolic was snappy
The rooters were happy
And Cleveland's bolt was shot

The games themselves were played in weather that Davis would describe as "fine weather for the humid race." It was weather apparently to the liking of the team as they went out and did what they had not done all year: win a doubleheader. Not only did they win, they won decisively, by 10–3 and 12–1 scores.

Shocker won the morning game, going all the way for his twenty-third victory, while Williams hit number thirty-three.

Sisler went four for four and he and Foster performed brilliantly in the field. When Foster came to bat for the first time he was given an ovation to mark his first appearance in St. Louis as a Brown.

In that first game the Browns jumped on Cleveland starter Jim Lindsey for four runs in the first inning. By the time he departed another four runs had been charged against him. The game would see the club collect fifteen hits and match that in the second game. In the latter contest Vangilder was finally restored to the starting rotation, and while he was touched for twelve hits, they produced only one run. Vangilder added to his prowess as a hitter by collecting his second home run of the season. Sisler picked up three hits in this game to go seven for nine for the day and extend his hitting streak to 34 games. Typical of both his and Foster's play that day was the handling of a hot grounder off the bat of Cleveland's Joe Wood. Foster raced to the foul line and with his bare hand stopped the ball. Without stopping to set himself he whirled and let the ball go. Sisler fastened his spike to the base and, reaching out far to his right, made the put-out. The double victory shaved a game from the New York lead as the Yankees were losing two to what some described as "their second team," the Boston Red Sox.

Despite Fohl's wish for no type of civic recognition at this time, management apparently conceded to go along with a team appearance at the previously mentioned Missouri Theater on September 5. The *Post-Dispatch* advertised that all the players would be present that night to receive testimonials from various St. Louis citizens. A better date could not have been picked as earlier in the day the Browns had pulled out a 10–9, eighth-inning victory to take first place for what would be the last time of the season. Another thing that proved to be a "last" would be an Urban Shocker pitching victory. This game marked his twenty-third win, and unfortunately, for St. Louis, there would be no more until the season's final weekend. The early innings had seen the Browns forge ahead and included Ken Williams' number 34 which came in the fourth with the bases loaded. Ray Kolp had started, but weakened in the sixth and was followed by Pruett, Wright, and Shocker, despite Shocker's appearance the day before. The Indians had rallied to lead the game 9–8 going into the Browns' eighth. The winning run can best be described in L. C. Davis' "The Thriller." The poem is reminiscent of the classic "Casey at the Bat":

The outlook wasn't brilliant for the Brownie boys that day
The Indians had uprisen in a most ferocious way
They donned their paint and feathers and unlimbered all their guns
And overwhelmed the Brownies who had led by seven runs

Then from ten thousand throats or more there issued urgent pleas
Five thousand had the willies and the rest had heart disease
Then up stepped Patrick Collins in the semifinal frame
And landing on the leather put the Brownies in the game

When a sacrifice by Tobin had advanced pinch runner Durst
On a "hit by pitcher" Foster took a journey down to first
The "Sis" beat out a bounder putting men on every base
And Williams flied to Connolly sending Durst across the base

And when the dust had settled there was Foster hugging third
While to a pitch of frenzy all the customers were stirred
On Sewell's chuck to center Eddie Foster crossed the pan
And the Yanks were running second while the Browns were in the van

Stockton was obviously ecstatic about the Browns' chances when he wrote: "Trouble in large quantities failed to squelch the fighting spirit of the pennant hungry Browns and when it appeared that the fine opportunity to take first place was about to be wasted, they rose in their might and smashed their way to victory."

And ecstatic he might be, as the lead held up the next day

with the Labor Day heroics returning for an 11–3 triumph. Davis pitched a strong game, giving Cleveland but seven hits. Williams continued his home run streak with number 34 while Jacobson added one of his own. The four-game sweep had featured 43 runs on 59 hits and complete games by Shocker, Vangilder, and Davis.

Thursday, September 7, was an open date before the start of a four-game series against Ty Cobb's Detroit Tigers. The city was in the throes of a pennant race that Stockton best describes:

> "How about the Browns?"
> "Have they really a chance?"
> "Do you think they'll cop that old pennant?"
> "Are they going to steam us up like this and then blow?"
> Everywhere you go you hear such questions. The barber asks the customer, the elevator man asks the newsboy, bank tellers can't cash a check without some gloomy or optimistic remarks. The butcher boy talks so much baseball he brings you the liver meant for the neighbor's bull pup. Caddies aren't worth their hire. They gather under each tree and are so busy arguing about the Browns that they lose a ball on every fairway. Conductors are so busy craning their necks at sports finals that they don't notice if you gave them last week's transfer or drop a cent into the box instead of a token.
> Baseball and the Browns have taken hold of the city. From now until the affair is settled one way or the other everything must be relegated to the classification of non-essential industry.

Stockton added this bit of prophecy which was to become all too true:

> The race is so close that it would not be surprising to see the flag won by the margin of one contest, nine innings, 27 put-outs, perhaps one run, one hit, one error. And if such should come to pass couldn't you make all the Browns feel bad by going back over the records and showing how a dozen games were thrown away, by pitchers and here and there by every man on the team?

First place was given up for the last time on September 8 when Detroit, led by Bobby Veach's two home runs off Urban Shocker, won an easy 8–3 victory. Meanwhile in New York the Yankees were defeating Washington 8–1. Both St. Louis streaks—Williams' home run effort and Sisler's consecutive hitting—were kept alive as Tiger first baseman Lu Blue pulled off two unassisted double plays. Both victimized Johnny Tobin and robbed him of likely base hits. The Browns could muster but five hits with Sisler, Jacobson, and Williams accounting for all of them. Perhaps more ominous were the eleven hits given up by Shocker before giving way to Wright in the ninth.

The bats came back the next day with a vengeance. The Browns pounded three Detroit pitchers for 20 hits which brought in 16 runs. Williams got the last of his current home run streak, number 37, while Vangilder allowed only five hits and came up with three of his own. Sisler went three for five and Jacobson collected three triples among his four hits. While a number of players have accomplished this feat since 1900, no one has yet hit four triples in a game. But the team stayed in second place as the Yankees won in ten innings over Washington.

Rain fell over St. Louis on Sunday, September 10, causing postponement of the third game of the Detroit series. But it did little to dampen the enthusiasm of the St. Louis fans. The Browns had announced the previous day that they would begin accepting World Series ticket applications. That announcement produced an avalanche of mail upon the team's offices at Spring Avenue and Dodier Street. On Sunday hundreds of special delivery requests were received, while the first delivery of mail on Monday morning brought two large sacks. The requests were filed in order of receipt with ticket distribution expected as soon as the Advisory Council of the National and American Leagues set prices.

While that distribution would never take place, the more immediate sale and distribution of tickets to the upcoming "Little World Series," as the press was touting the coming decisive three-game set with the Yankees, was of most immediate concern to Bob Quinn. The games were scheduled for Saturday, September 16; Sunday, September 17; and Monday, September 18. Tickets were placed on sale at 9 a.m. from a cigar store at 409 Olive Street. The first customer arrived at 6:30 a.m., and by 11:00 a.m. there were 576 in a line that extended for two and one-half blocks. By noon the Saturday and Sunday tickets had been exhausted. A wait of three and one-half hours was not uncommon.

The rain-out gave the *Post-Dispatch* staff an opportunity to do some relevant sidebars. Joseph Holland talked with Detroit manager Ty Cobb, who felt the home field advantage and "breaks" would give the Browns an advantage over New York, which had to close the season with a tough Western swing. He included this bit of prophecy in his analysis: "I mean the Browns, due to the new strain of a pennant fight, may miss an important play at a vital stage. They may make errors when they cost ball games. Errors cannot be helped, but they always hurt. That is what I mean when I say the Browns may beat themselves in some games, just as Detroit has beaten itself many times through inexperience or one slight misstep."

Herman Weche made a detailed study of the Brown's pitching staff and came to the unsurprising conclusion that Shocker was the only ace on the team:

> Shocker has proven the "Ironman" of the local pitching staff. He has gone the route 27 times, 11 more than Elam Vangilder, who ranks second in finishing what he starts. Only nine times has Fohl been forced to send a pitcher to Shocker's rescue. That's real flinging in these days of the lively ball, but the spitter's record shows just what a real hurler is able to do. . . .
>
> Statistics show that in 69 of the games played by the Browns up to and including last Wednesday's contest, which resulted in a victory over Cleveland, the pitcher who started went the route. That shows that in 67, or one half of the team's battles, Fohl was forced to call in a relief man.

Sports editor John Wray echoed Weche's thoughts in his own column:

> It is patent that, despite the good looking records of some of the club's pitchers, there is only one hurler in whom the fans have solid confidence – Urban Shocker. . . . In 67 games the Browns have had to send in relief hurlers – that tells the story of the staff. They are 50 per cent hurlers. That is to say, it's fifty-fifty whether they pitch well or poorly, on any specific day. . . .

Play resumed on Monday with the Browns pulling out one of their most spectacular victories of the season. Detroit had built a 4–3 lead on "Dixie" Davis, but Pruett had shut the door on the Tigers after the fifth inning. Howard Ehmke retired Pat Collins, pinch-hitting for Pruett, and Johnny Tobin to lead off the Browns' ninth. When he then got two strikes on Foster, the 17,000 spectators started for the exits. But Foster worked the count to 3–2 before being given first base by rookie umpire Guthrie on a close call. That brought up George Sisler. Ty Cobb, sensing trouble, replaced the slow-footed "Fats" Fothergill in right field with the speedy Ira Flagstead. It mattered not. Sisler slammed the ball between right and center and wound up on third as Foster scored the tying run. Ehmke intentionally walked Williams and unintentionally did the same to Jacobson to load the bases. McManus then lined a single to center to score Sisler with the winning run. Some spectators rushed on the field and lifted McManus to their shoulders and carried him halfway to the dugout. It was a grand victory, but the Yankees also won and the standings remained the same.

It was also a disastrous victory. In the seventh inning Cobb grounded to short and Gerber made a wide throw on the otherwise routine ball. Sisler stretched so far to the right to get the ball that he fell forward onto his shoulder, bruising the muscle severely. Nothing was made of the incident at the time, and Sisler played out the game. But he failed to appear for the final game of the Detroit series. Fohl inserted Jacobson at first as the game got underway while Shorten took center. Then in the second inning Sisler appeared, remarking in jest that his tardiness was due to a banquet appearance the night before. In reality the shoulder had caused him such pain that sleep was impossible, and the Browns superstar had spent the morning consulting various specialists. He could not raise his arm above his shoulder.

Neither Fohl nor Quinn had had any previous knowledge of the problem, and they were at first unable to answer the numerous queries from the crowd. As the situation clarified itself, spectators sitting behind the Browns dugout passed the word about Sisler's condition. The word-of-mouth report spread quickly around Sportsman's Park. Later, Dr. Robert Hyland, the team physician, issued the following medical bulletin as reported by *Post-Dispatch* sports editor John Wray:

> Sisler is suffering from a severe and extremely painful strain of the deltoid muscle of the right shoulder which he experienced in Monday's play against Detroit. Movement of the arm caused him so much misery that I immobilized the arm and shoulder in tape and have ordered him to keep it so for a week.
>
> Sisler does not think the injury is of much consequence. He would like to try playing in two or three days. If he does it may make his trouble worse. I feel that Sisler will be very fortunate to completely recover before the close of the season, though he doubtless will try to play. For one week it is certain he ought not to attempt anything on the ball field, but I guess he will try to get into the Yankee series despite my advice.

Not only did the Browns now face the prospect of going into the biggest series of the pennant race against the Yankees without their star player, Sisler himself stood to lose some individual goals. He was now one game short of tying Ty Cobb's modern era hitting streak of 40 consecutive games (ironically, his injury had occurred on a play involving Cobb). In 1920 Sisler had compiled 257 hits, a major league record that still stands, and had he played in all of the remaining games of 1922 it is likely that he would have established a new record.

But Sisler was not only the quintessential team player; many called him the perfect player. It took W. C. Fields, the booze-loving comedian, to find a flaw. Fields was a fan of both baseball and Sisler. Once when the Browns were in Boston while the comedy star was appearing there, he invited Sisler to visit him backstage

at the Majestic Theater. The ensuing conversation was later recounted in the *New York Times* as part of Sisler's obituary:

> "You fascinate me, George," commented Fields. "I've admired your artistry very much many times. Have a drink."
> "No thanks, I don't drink," replied Sisler.
> Pouring one for himself Fields reflected: "Well, even the perfect ballplayer can't have everything."

Perhaps not everything, but pretty close. Geroge Harold Sisler was born March 24, 1893, at Nimisila, near Akron, Ohio. Both his father, Cassius, and mother, Mary, were graduates of Hiram College. Sisler continued the academic tradition by entering the University of Michigan in 1911. At Michigan he met Branch Rickey, then serving as baseball coach, and established a relationship that would last half a century. But before entering Michigan Sisler was the center of a controversy that was to have far-reaching effects upon the structure of organized baseball.

When he was 17 Sisler signed a minor league contract with the Akron team. He received no money and never played a game, preferring to go on to Michigan. The Pittsburgh Pirates ultimately acquired the contract, but Sisler followed Rickey, who had gone on to the Browns, upon graduation in 1915. The problem of which team Sisler was under contract to was thrown into the lap of the then three-man National Commission that ruled major league baseball. The commission was composed of National League president John Tener, his American League counterpart, Ban Johnson, and Cincinnati Reds owner Garry Hermann. The commission voted 2–1, Hermann siding with Johnson, to award Sisler to the Browns because the original contract was signed when he was a minor. Pirates owner Barney Dreyfuss was enraged and neither forgave nor forgot. He constantly attacked the commission until the Black Sox scandal hit and led to the establishment of the position of commissioner of baseball, the system that exists to this day.

***Opposite:* The greatest Brown of them all, George Sisler. Sisler led the American League in hitting with a .420 average in 1922. (Photo courtesy of the *St. Louis Post-Dispatch*.)**

At Michigan Rickey had used Sisler in the outfield and on the mound. When he reported to the Browns at Comiskey Park in Chicago in June 1915, Rickey had changed his mind. Two days later he started his first game at first base. Sisler also did some pitching that first year, defeating his boyhood idol Walter Johnson 2–1, and winding up the season with a 4–5 record and a solid .285 average. But like his contemporary, Ruth, his hitting ability was such as to abolish any thought of a pitching career. In 1916, his first full season, he hit .305 as the regular first baseman. The year 1917 saw Sisler emerge as a genuine superstar with a .353 average, which was followed by .341 a year later and .352 in 1919. Not only was he an outstanding hitter, who felt any average below .350 was poor, he was a superb fielder and outstanding base stealer. Standing only 5′ 11″ and weighing 170 pounds, "Gorgeous George," as he was also known, combined extraordinary reflexes with great speed to become simply one of the finest players in the history of the sport.

If baseball thought that they had seen the best of "The Sizzler"–another nickname–the 1920–22 timeframe was to be his very best. Over that three-year period he collected 719 hits, scored 396 runs, and stole 128 bases while posting successive batting averages of .407, .371, and .420. The two .400 marks were good enough to win batting titles. He also led in stolen bases in 1921 and 1922 as well as runs scored in 1922. As previously mentioned, Sisler got 257 hits in 1920, but despite that was prouder of the fact that his 19 home runs were more than any other player except Ruth had garnered in a single season. He always regarded his pitching victory over Walter Johnson as the greatest thrill of his career.

There are countless incidents of exceptional ability in the career of a player with the stature of George Sisler. But it does well to recount here a sampling of these:

1. In 1916 in a game against Boston, the Red Sox had runners on first and third with none out. The next hitter sent a routine fly ball to left fielder Burt Shotton. Conceding the run, Shotton threw to Sisler to get the runner returning to first. Making the

put-out, Sisler whirled and threw to Severeid at the plate for a triple play.

2. He once fielded a ground ball deep behind the bag. Running forward, he lobbed the ball toward the pitcher, who was moving to cover. Realizing that the pitcher wouldn't get there in time, he simply accelerated in time to make the catch and put-out himself.

3. Earlier in the 1922 season against Washington, Joe Judge was on third and Roger Peckinpaugh was batting for the Senators. Peckinpaugh bunted down the first base line. Sisler had bolted with the pitch and, scooping up the ball 15 feet from home plate, tagged Peckinpaugh coming down the line, then threw to Severeid to get Judge at the plate.

But Sisler was now out of action, and L. C. Davis lamented the fact in his "Tough Luck":

> The Cards have first basemen galore
> And still to the front they can't forge
> The Browns had but one
> And at present have none
> Oh, why should the fates pick up George?

Going into the seventh inning of their first Sisler-less game since early August, the Browns trailed Detroit 5–3. Fohl started Kolp, but the Tigers got to him for four runs before the end of the third inning. Kolp apparently put too many right over the plate, something that Frank Ellerbe recalled he had an aversion to in practice: "Old Ray Kolp . . . in hitting practice he wouldn't throw a ball over the middle of the plate for me for anything. He'd throw them a little lopsided, inside, one or the other. I said, 'Throw it over here, Ray. I won't hit it back at you. I'll pull it. I'll pull it.'"

Vangilder relieved and pitched well until the ninth. The Browns had rallied to take an 8–5 lead into Detroit's last inning. In the eighth, with Shorten at first, Tiger pitcher George Dauss elected to intentionally walk Ken Williams. But the American League home run leader foiled that by reaching across the plate and sending the third wide delivery into left for a base hit. Jacobson followed with a single, and the Browns had the lead. But in the ninth Detroit got to Vangilder for one run, had a runner at third and Cobb at the plate. After throwing three wide ones at Cobb, Vangilder was yanked, and Fohl brought in Pruett for more heroics. The rookie lefthander, who was being written off for the remainder of the season a few weeks previous, was now the savior. He proceeded to strike out Cobb and Veach and got Fothergill to fly to Williams to end the game. With the Yankees idle, the victory drew the Browns to within a game of first.

Despite the victory, Jacobson had not played well at first base, making two errors. Fohl moved McManus there, shifted Foster to second base, and returned Ellerbe to third for the opening game of the Red Sox series on September 13. The game marked Ellerbe's first appearance since his knee problem sidelined him on July 19. But none of the changes mattered; despite Shocker's five-hit pitching, the Red Sox won 3–1. Shocker was working his last start before the upcoming "Little World Series" with the Yankees and pitched brilliantly to everyone except George Burns. The Red Sox first baseman hammered a Shocker offering into the left field seats with one on, and that proved to be the margin of defeat. The Yankees were splitting a doubleheader in Chicago and increased their lead to one and a half games.

The medical reports on Sisler were still pessimistic and few, other than himself, thought he would be ready for New York.

McManus had made an error in the first Red Sox game which led to a run and to Pat Collins taking over at first base. Collins was normally Severeid's back-up and hit well whenever inserted into the lineup. McManus went back to second and Foster to third for the second game of the Boston series. It was another of the now familiar Browns comebacks. Davis started, and when walks he issued in the first and third innings led to runs, Fohl brought in Wright. The Browns tied the score in the seventh and went ahead to win 5–3 in the eighth. Jacobson's triple, Severied's single, and Gerber's double produced the win, which went to Kolp in relief. Collins, true to form, had three singles in four appearances and played well at first base.

The Browns closed to within a half-game of the Yankees on September 15 when they again pulled off a late rally to defeat Boston 7–1. Vangilder went the distance, giving only five hits and no bases on balls. Still St. Louis trailed 1–0 after six and a half innings before a five-run rally decided the issue in the seventh. The victory coupled with the New York loss to the White Sox brought the Browns to within a half-game of first place on the eve of the season's biggest series.

The week had seen an avalanche of ticket applications for what St. Louis hoped would be its first World Series. In addition to requests received on Sunday by special delivery, Monday's mail had brought an estimated 10,000 letters. Ten clerks worked in a large room under the Sportsman's Park grandstand to process the workload.

"There already is plenty of gossip, chiefly to the effect favored persons will get the tickets," Quinn told the *Post-Dispatch*. "That is not true. I have heard the rumor that one undertaker already has 2000 tickets in his safe. How absurd! The tickets are not yet printed for the price has not been set by the Baseball Commission."

As the weekend drew near, ticket attention shifted to the immediate pennant-deciding games with the Yankees. Tickets for the Sunday game, normally $1.50 for reserved and $1.25 for boxes, were being scalped for $15 each. All such seats had long ago been sold out.

George Sisler's condition was another matter of concern to all of St. Louis. On Friday it was reported that his shoulder was greatly improved and there was a chance that he would play the following day. Dr. Hyland thought it unwise for him to do so, fearing more serious injury, but conceded Sisler's competitive spirit would no doubt rule out any practical considerations. Sisler would of course play, though he would later tell Tom Meany in *Baseball's Greatest Hitters*:

> Actually I should never have played. The arm was so badly crippled that I had to lift my gloved hand with my left in order to catch balls at first base. I told the guys to be sure and throw the ball low and I couldn't possibly catch a ball over my head. At bat, I was practically one handed. It was ridiculous for me to even try to play but I was young then and you couldn't have kept me out of there with a gun.

The line began to form for the Saturday game at 11 p.m. on Friday. By midnight more had joined the long vigil for grandstand, bleacher, and on-the-field locations in Sportsman's Park. At 10 a.m. on the big day, Saturday, September 16, there were some 600 people in line at both the grandstand and bleacher windows. By 11:30 a.m. fans were standing four abreast west on Dodier Street to Spring Avenue and west to Grand Boulevard. The line from the bleacher windows stretched along Grand Boulevard from Sullivan to Dodier and doubled back until it reached Sullivan again.

The series had captured the imagination of Midwestern baseball fans. Among those in line who had come by automobile in an attempt to see the culmination of the American League pennant race were people from not only Missouri, but Illinois, Iowa, Arkansas, and western Indiana. One group had come from as far as Junction City, Kansas, having left there on Thursday. Another pair of fans from Oklahoma City came up by train and willingly paid $45 for two reserved seats. Scalpers were getting $25 and $30 each for box seats along the field. Such scalping was not uncommon, but was not seen in the vicinity of the park. Perhaps it was because the St. Louis police were there in full force to control the crowd and enforce special parking regulations. Two lieutenants, five sergeants, 65 patrolmen, eight mounted officers, and six motorcycle policemen were on duty.

It was not planned for the gates to be opened until 12:30 for the 3:00 game, but Quinn gave the word at 11:45 to let the crowd into the park. Quinn had originally estimated that some 25,000 would view the first game, but that figure was quickly upped to 30,000 as the masses surged into the park. While no turnstile count was possible, it was evident that a new attendance record was established, exceeding the 29,508 that had paid to see the Sunday game in the city series with the Cardinals the previous April. Both pavilions, the entire upper deck of the grandstand and the bleachers, with the exception of a few poor seats in center field, were filled by 1:00 p.m. At 1:10 the gates leading from the bleachers were opened and many fans rushed for good viewing points behind the ropes that were stretched from one end of the bleachers to the other on the field. The mounted officers had some difficulty with the crowd behind the ropes and needed help from patrolmen on foot to maintain order. The crowd here was estimated at about 2,000, while several hundred fans were also seated in temporary locations in the front of each pavilion.

The crowd had fortified itself during the long wait with the usual ball park fare of hot dogs, peanuts, etc., but once inside there were other diversions before the game got underway. A U.S. Army dirigible cruised over the northwestern portion of the city. The Pennant Boosters Club gave away 1,000 small horns and 3,600 pieces of literature to stimulate enthusiasm; they had also arranged to have six cheerleaders present. While the crowd did not respond to the organized aspect of the cheering, the horns were well used. Other fans had cowbells and took great delight in shaking them and shouting "Tom Mix" and "Bill Hart" (cowboy stars of the era) when mounted police were in the area.

Frequently, particular individuals provided comic relief. One woman was seen racing to her seat in the grandstand with a hot dog in her right hand, a seat cushion in her left, and a scorecard between her teeth. While the Browns' reserves took batting practice, one of the firemen assigned to the park retrieved the ball when necessary and returned it to the pitcher. When one of the hitters lofted a foul fly, the fireman waved off the players to make the catch, only to miss it – to the delight of those watching. Joey Ryan had come in from Terre Haute for the big series and participated in fungo batting with the team's bat boys. The official announcer came out during batting practice to announce through his megaphone: "John Smith is wanted at his office." This call for a John Smith among 30,000, where there were more than a few John Smiths, brought smiles to the faces of many.

Fohl had first the regulars and then the reserves out for batting practice. Jimmy Austin got a big hand when he stepped to the mound to pitch. George Sisler did not immediately take part, but was in the dugout in uniform. There was a great cheer from the crowd as Sisler emerged from the dugout and went to the plate. Just then the Yankees made their appearance on the field and the cheers turned to jeers. Sisler took two swings at the ball and connected on both, appearing to be back to normal. Photographers quickly got him aside after his batting and photographed him in various poses. Sisler was not the only one with a health problem. Johnny Tobin was suffering from a severe cold, but still managed to put one in the right field bleachers during the practice. Sisler took two more swings, connecting both times, before returning to the dugout.

As usual, the center of attention for New York was Ruth. The crowd was delighted when he swung and missed during batting practice. So delighted in fact that some threw straw hats on the field, a custom of the times. Ruth simply drove the next one out on to Grand Boulevard. The photographers turned their attention to the Yankees while Browns fans asked each other who could possibly care after their team won the pennant.

Lending further to the World Series atmosphere, American League president Ban Johnson had assigned three umpires, Billy Evans, Bill Dineen, and Bill Guthrie, to work the games. Today that is one short of the normal crew, while six umpires work World Series and All-Star games, but two officials were the usual complement for the regular season games in this era.

The Browns took the field to a deafening roar, Shocker took his four warm-up pitches (they take eight today), Whitey Witt stepped into the box, and the "Little World Series" was underway. Shocker got Witt to drop a slow roller to Foster, and he proceeded to beat it out for a single. Dugan then threw a real scare into the crowd by lining to center for what looked like a sure double, but Williams made a great running catch for the out. Shocker settled down and retired the side.

Miller Huggins started Bob Shawkey, and the choice was an excellent one. Shawkey would give the Browns only seven hits—all but one somewhat tainted—strike out five, and give up no walks. Shocker was almost as good, but not quite, surrendering nine hits, striking out six, and walking two.

The Yankees struck first in the second inning. Meusel singled to center and took second when Jacobson bobbled the ball. Ward sacrificed him to third, and Everett Scott's single brought him home. The Yankees were back with another in the third. Dugan singled to left and Ruth followed with one to right, putting Dugan on third. Pipp then flied to Williams in left and just barely beat the accurate throw to the plate. New York led 2–0.

The Browns made some noise, but not quite enough, in the sixth. Gerber led off with a roller to Ward, who should have made the play for a put-out. Shocker then grounded to Ward, who fumbled the ball long enough to retire only the pitcher rather than getting a double play. Tobin followed with one of his classic bunt singles. Ward handled Tobin's bunt, but was unable to make a play at any base. Thus the bases were loaded for St. Louis, thanks to Aaron Ward, but the Yankee second baseman had not been charged with an error. Nor would he be charged with an error when Foster next grounded to him and once again the ball skidded between his legs. Gerber came home with the Browns' first run and Foster was credited with a base hit. That would be enough to unnerve most pitchers, but Shawkey was equal to the task. Sisler, who had extended his hitting streak to 40 games by doubling off the unfortunate Ward's shins in the fourth to tie Cobb's record, was the next hitter. He sent what appeared to be a sure single in the direction of none other than Ward again. A hit would have scored two runs and put the Browns ahead, but Ward finally rose to the occasion. In this game the simple plays gave him problems: the difficult were executed brilliantly. Ward made a desperate lunge on his bare-hand side and made the stop. He flipped to Scott for one and over to Pipp, and the Yankees were out of the inning.

The game probably would have been remembered as one which New York won in spite of Aaron Ward except for an historic and ugly incident in the ninth inning. The Browns got Severeid to second in the eighth, when Ward muffed the catcher's grounder. Once again an error was not charged. Gerber then sacrificed Severeid along, but then Shawkey struck out Shocker and Tobin to end the inning. The Yankees went out in their half of the ninth, and the Browns came up for the last time.

Foster led off and lifted a fly to right center. Bob Meusel, the right fielder, and Lawton "Whitey" Witt, the center fielder, moved to make the catch. Just as Meusel was about to take it, a bottle came flying through the air and struck Witt on the forehead. Whether it came from the bleachers or the crowd behind the ropes was never definitely determined, but Witt crumbled and fell to the ground. After the fall the spectators reached him before the New York players arrived on the scene. There was no ill intent on the part of the crowd, and they sought to give the unconscious player aid. But players from both teams, umpires, and mounted police were soon there. Witt was carried to the Yankee clubhouse by reserve catcher Fred "Bootnose" Hoffman. The New York center fielder had suffered a slight brain concussion and was revived and treated by the Browns' team physician, Dr. Hyland.

Meusel did make the catch for the first out, but the incident changed the mood of the crowd noticeably. The *Post-Dispatch* observed:

> There were shouts of "Call the game, we've seen enough," and "Give the game to New York and let's go home." A great majority of the spectators gave every manifestation of sympathy for the injured player and some even went to extravagant lengths to make at least verbal amends.
>
> ...When at last the excitement caused by the bottle throwing had died down sufficiently to let the game go on Sisler went to bat. And hundreds in the grandstand crowd set up a cry the like of which was never before heard in St. Louis. They clamored for Bob Shawkey, the New York pitcher, to strike Sisler out.

> Of course, this was in the heat of intense excitement and there were many who tried to counteract it by shouting encouragement to Sisler, but it was apparent that many in the crowd had lost their enthusiasm for a Browns' victory. Some openly said that the sickening effect of the assault on Witt had left them with no desire other than to see the game quickly terminated. With a heat which probably will be tempered by reflection later, a man in the reserved seat section who had been rooting vigorously for the Browns exclaimed: "I'm through with baseball. I don't care who wins the pennant now."

The game was ended quickly enough. Sisler tapped the ball weakly for a bunt and was thrown out easily. Kenneth Williams knocked an easy fly to right field. The victory was New York's. After the game Sisler told a *Post-Dispatch* reporter that the bottle throwing incident "had taken the heart out of the Browns" and in its effect on the players had destroyed any chance for a ninth-inning rally to win the game.

A report gained wide circulation that a shower of bottles was seen around Witt before he fell. This was not borne out by investigation, and interviews obtained from witnesses mention one or at most two bottles. Manager Huggins of the New York team exhibited one bottle with the assertion that it was the one that hit Witt. Several spectators who were on the field said they saw a bottle hit Witt and another go over his head as he was falling.

Witt's injury was not serious, but as in Sisler's case, Dr. Hyland urged caution. He told the *Post-Dispatch*: "The blow from the bottle caused a severe contusion and laceration of the forehead and slight concussion of the brain. The injury was not serious, but it would not be advisable for Witt to play before Monday."

As might be expected Witt would have none of this. He responded:

> I believe I will be able to play tomorrow. Although my doctor said I suffered a slight concussion of the brain, I do not believe it severe enough to keep me out of the game.

> I did not see the bottle before it struck me. I was running toward the crowd from which the bottle was thrown when it struck me square in the forehead. It literally knocked me off my feet.

The attack appeared to solidify the Yankees, who had been wracked by dissension throughout the season. Team members were genuinely concerned with Witt's condition and clamored around him in the club house: "How are you, Whitey, my boy? Does it hurt much? Never mind, lad we'll whip 'em for you tomorrow." Miller Huggins expressed optimism that that was what exactly might happen: "If we can win tomorrow we've got 'em whipped, boys."

The *Post-Dispatch* covered the incident extensively and recorded the reactions of a number of those close to the scene. Umpire Billy Evans, who had himself been the victim of a similar attack in St. Louis in 1907, said:

> The bottle that struck Witt was the only one I saw thrown and was evidently tossed by some fanatic. I do not think anyone should take the act as representative of the crowd. After the incident there was an appalling silence that indicated strong disapproval of the act. St. Louis grandstands are usually very fair.

Col. Tillinghast H. Huston, one of the New York owners:

> It was a very unfair attack and in a decided contrast to the wonderful behavior and good sportsmanship of the big crowd. But the New York players do not hold the vicious act of one person against the St. Louis fans.

Phil Ball, the Browns' owner:

> It was a most deplorable incident. It took the "pep" out of me altogether. I have offered a reward of $500 for the arrest and conviction of the person who threw the bottle. As a step toward the prevention of a recurrence of such tactics, I have

> issued orders that hereafter no soda in bottles will be sold on the field. When there is an overflow crowd the fans on the field will have to do without soda in bottles.

The St. Louis Pennant Boosters' Club:

> The St. Louis Pennant Boosters' Club deplores the incident which occurred to "Whitey" Witt, New York outfielder, when he was hit by a fan in today's game.

Almost lost in the concern for Witt and the distaste for the bottle throwing act was George Sisler's condition. *Post-Dispatch* writer Dent McSkimming was in the St. Louis clubhouse after the game when Phil Ball inquired as to his first baseman's health:

> "It's aching terribly, now. The doctor tells me that the injured muscle is trying to contract, now after all that loosening up exercise during the game, and that's what pains so," responded Sisler.
>
> "Will you be in the game Sunday?" asked Ball.
>
> "Sure I'll try to play. The shoulder ought to feel better by tomorrow."

There was conjecture that if Sisler's shoulder had been 100 percent he would have beaten the throw to first, allowing the tying run to score, back in the sixth inning. His arm had hung limply at his side, reducing the speed generated by the normal swinging of the arm on the dash to first base.

The loss put the Browns back by a game and a half and made victory on Sunday virtually mandatory if they were to remain in the race. It seemed an appropriate time to call on the Almighty for assistance, and that may be what Foster, Ellerbe, and Durst had in mind when they visited the Sunday School class of the Centenary Methodist Church prior to the game. The pastor, the Reverend C. W. Tadlock, introduced the trio to prolonged cheers and promised a Browns victory in the pennant race. (There is no indication of what authority gave the Reverend Tadlock that revelation!) Foster, who was a member of the church's adult Bible class, and the others presented autographed baseballs to two students who had won an attendance contest.

At Sportsman's Park the fans arrived even earlier than the prior day. The bottle throwing incident had prompted the St. Louis police to throw tighter lines around the crowd standing in the outfield. Officers and plainclothesmen were also in the bleachers and ejected one fan for berating Umpire Guthrie. Still in the early going the spectators seemed subdued. When "Whitey" Witt came to bat for the first time wearing a bandage around his head, he received a generous ovation. However, as the game proceeded the partisan nature of the home crowd inevitably showed through, pop bottle incident nowithstanding. In the eighth inning when New York manager Miller Huggins sent McMillan in to hit for the pitcher, the fans in center field waived their white handkerchiefs to add to the already poor background formed by the sea of white shirts. The police and Ken Williams forced them to stop.

It was another 30,000 throng that witnessed what some have described as the Browns' highwater mark, not only for this season, but for their entire 52-year history. The *New York Times* observed:

> Phil Ball and his minions defied all the laws of physics, and packed even more people into the park today than had been jammed in yesterday. Where the extra room came from will always be a profound mystery....
>
> The grandstand and bleachers all had the people in them that the law would allow. Folks stood on tiptoes at the back of the stand. In the bleachers youngsters straddled the fence and clung to the base of the flag pole. A few sturdy souls even climbed to the roof of a small bleacher near the end of the first base foul line, and maintained a precarious perch on the smooth, sharp-sloping roof....
>
> It is regrettable to report, however, that the official cheerleaders were missing. The crowd had to get along on its own hook and it did beautifully. Everybody was armed with a horn and a rattler with which to agitate the atmosphere. Shrieking humanity was everywhere, on all sides of the field, even within reach of the players' benches....

Fohl started Pruett, who, while he had completed only three games all season, had been a most effective relief pitcher in the games leading up to the "Little World Series." His mid-season arm problems appeared to be behind him and he was, of course, the most effective pitcher of all time against Ruth. Huggins went with another of his aces, "Schoolboy" Waite Hoyt. Whatever intercession Foster and the others had with the Almighty worked wonders through the vehicle of Pruett's left arm. He proceeded to:

Give only one base on balls.
Strike out eight.
Throw 103 pitches in nine innings.
Pitch 20 called strikes, one for every four other balls thrown.
Pitch a total of 48 strikes and foul strikes, almost one for every other ball thrown.
Allow only nine balls to the outfield, six of which went for putouts.
Allow but five hits, one questionable.

He faltered only in the Yankee sixth when Ruth, for the only time in his career, sent one of his offerings into Grand Boulevard for a short-lived 1–0 lead. In the home half of the inning Foster walked and Sisler followed with a single, establishing a new major league record for hitting in 41 consecutive games. It broke Cobb's existing record and stood until Joe DiMaggio's 56-game streak was established in 1941. The streak has been passed on other occasions, most recently by Pete Rose in 1978. George Sisler, Jr., commented: "Dad had no feeling that hitting in 30-40-50 consecutive games was any great accomplishment. Many times he told me he never went to bat without expecting to get a hit. I am sure he would have been happy for Rose if Pete regarded his streak as noteworthy."

Foster stopped at second on Sisler's hit and came in with the tying run when Williams singled over Yankee first baseman Wally Pipp's head. Sisler advanced to third on the play and after

McManus struck out, Severeid singled to center, scoring both Sisler and Williams. The latter had previously stolen second. The Browns carried the 3–1 lead into their half of the eighth. Huggins had yanked Hoyt and sent in "Sad Sam" Jones, normally a starter. Foster walked, but was caught stealing. That hardly mattered when Sisler also walked and Williams hit his thirty-eighth home run into the right field seats for a 5–1 lead.

But there was still some drama to come. Pruett gave up consecutive singles to Dugan and Ruth to lead off the New York ninth. Dugan went to third when Pipp forced Ruth at second. The rookie lefthander then ran the count to 3–2 on Yankee catcher Wally Schang before getting him swinging as Severeid doubled up Pipp, who was on his way to second. The Browns were back to a half-game deficit. Pruett was carried from the field on the shoulders of St. Louis fandom, who had now long forgotten their remorse over the Witt incident.

Interviewed by the *Post-Dispatch* afterward, Pruett would say:

> My arm felt fine all the way. It was stronger than ever before and I had not the slightest twinge of pain as I felt at the time that my arm went bad, two months ago.
>
> I can truthfully say that I never felt better in pitching any game. Control, of course, helped me a great deal. It minimized the pitching effort and thus saved me from going clear "out" on every pitch.

The drama of the occasion was perfect for an L. C. Davis poem, "The Battle of the Schoolboys":

When Schoolboy Pruett took the hill
  Determined on a great exploit
He found he'd have to hurl the pill
  Against the famous Schoolboy Hoyt
And it was up to Hoyt and Pruett
  To show their elders how to do it.

The Brownies couldn't get to Waite
  The Yankees couldn't get to "Shucks"
They put the ball across the plate
  And fooled the heavy hitting ducks
It was like there was nothing to it
  But Mr. Hoyt and Mr. Pruett.

As to and fro the battle raged
  Terrific was the mental strain
No batting rallies had been staged
  And neither side an inch could gain
For Hoyt was there to make them rue it
  As was the young and gallant Pruett.

The fans were straining at the ropes
  And madly cheering for the Browns
The while their cherished pennant hopes
  Were having many ups and downs
While Yankee batters gazed at Pruett
  And marveled at the way he threw it.

The Yanks had scored a single run
  Which proved to be their only tally
And in the sixth the Brownies won
  By putting on a batting rally
And in the end the Yankees blew it
  Because they couldn't get to Pruett.

No, they couldn't get to Pruett on Sunday, but Monday was to be another story, when the epic of the 1922 St. Louis Browns would be played out to what would be its ultimate conclusion.

Crowdwise it was Saturday and Sunday all over again. By noon when the gates were thrown open, the number of fans in the lines was such as to immediately fill the 3600 seats in the upper tier of the grandstand and more than half-fill the first base side pavilion. One hour before game time the only vacant seating was the reserved section, whose lucky occupants could afford to bide their time. The throng in the outfield, which had been deprived of its white handerkerchief ploy, thought of a new wrinkle to antagonize New York hitters: They locked arms and swayed back and forth to provide a moving white background!

Bill Bayne's name appeared in the scorecard for the game, and the possibility of his being the starter was given further credence when Fohl indicated that he might go with a long shot. Lefthander Pruett had baffled the Yankees with his fadeaway; perhaps Bayne, also a southpaw, might be able to solve New York. But when the time came for the game to get under way it was Frank T. "Dixie" Davis who went to the hill. Huggins went with "Bullet Joe" Bush, who had pitched an inning of relief the day before. Bush was noted for his forkball – actually a curveball, but so called because the two-fingered grip resembled a fork.

George Sisler was once again at first, Fohl evidently reasoning that half a Sisler was better than a whole substitute. His lack of mobility was evident in the Yankee first when, after Witt had singled and Dugan and Ruth had gone out, Gerber threw wide to him on Pipp's routine grounder. Sisler dropped the ball and Witt went to third. Fortunately Davis got the next hitter to line to McManus and the inning was over.

Jacobson averted another possible New York run in the fourth when Pipp hit a potential double to right center. The crowd opened up nicely for "Jake," and he leaned over some fans to make the catch. Huggins protested vigorously over this, but got nowhere. The Yankees were not so nicely treated in the fifth when Jacobson himself flied to center. Witt went back for the catch, but the crowd stood its ground and the ball fell in for a double. McManus then singled, but Jacobson held up at third. He then scored the first run of the game on Severeid's sacrifice fly.

The Browns led 1–0 after five innings, but both Davis and Bush were pitching at their limits. Davis had given up only two hits, and Bush had matched that performance. The Browns got another single in the sixth and finally broke through for another run and two hits in the seventh. In that inning Ken Williams dropped a double into the right field crowd to lead off. After Jacobson sacrificed him to third, McManus got a ground rule double of his own into left field and Williams crossed the plate to make it 2–0. Bush then retired the side and New York came to bat in the top of the eighth.

It was to be the beginning of the end. With two out and Dugan on second via a double, Pipp singled off Davis' glove. McManus threw wildly to first, allowing Dugan to score the Yankees' first run. Davis then struck out Meusel to end the inning, but the lead was now only 2–1. McManus' error proved to be an ill omen. Bush set the Browns down in order and New York came up for the last time in the top of the ninth. The Browns were the proverbial "three outs away," in this case from a half-game lead in the pennant race, but many felt from the pennant itself.

Perhaps it might have been worse if Davis had retired the first two hitters and had then run into trouble. But the problems started immediately. The lead-off hitter in the inning, Wally Schang, sent one back to Davis which bounced off his glove. Before he could recover, Schang was at first base with an infield single. Huggins then sent lefthand-hitting Elmer Smith up to hit for Aaron Ward. Davis' first pitch got away from Severeid for a passed ball, and Schang was now in scoring position. Fohl called time, and a lengthy conference was held at the mound. Fohl was fearful of the lefthand-hitting Smith against the righthanded Davis. Davis was as strong as ever; Schang's glove hit could have come off any pitcher, and he wanted to finish the game. But Fohl made the decision that would be second-guessed for the rest of his life. Davis came out, and Pruett came in. Huggins then simply sent right-handed hitter Mike McNally up to hit for Smith. McNally attempted to sacrifice Schang to third and dropped a bunt in front of the plate. Severeid pounced on it as he had so many other times, but in the heat of battle his throw to Foster at third in an attempt to get Schang was low and wide. Foster had to make a great effort to keep it from getting past him. Schang was now at third, McNally at first, and none were out.

Still Pruett had been consistently effective in relief, and though he was no doubt tired from his previous nine-inning effort, Fohl felt he had that little extra left. He changed his mind about that after Pruett walked Everett Scott to load the bases. There was really no one else to turn to now but the old master, Urban Shocker. And so Shocker came on and momentarily turned the tide. Joe Bush was the next Yankee hitter, and Huggins let him bat. He was an excellent hitter and had pitched an outstanding game. Bush grounded to McManus, who this time threw accurately to the plate to get Schang coming in from third. One out. But look who's hitting now: "Whitey" Witt, the victim of the Saturday bottle throwing incident. Irony of ironies – and Witt took full advantage of it. He singled sharply to center, scoring both McNally and Scott, and New York led for the first time, 3–2. The cliche says, "It's all over but the shouting," but there was no shouting. This was St. Louis, and the stands were silent.

Shocker got Dugan to hit into a double play to end the inning, but there would be no miracle for the Browns in their half of the ninth. Sisler grounded out to McNally, who was now at second for the Yankees. This ended his hitting streak, as Bush had earlier gotten him to ground out to both the second baseman and shortstop, as well as popping up to Dugan. Now it was Williams' turn. One of his patented drives would tie the score and conceivably send the game into extra innings. The best Williams could do was pop up to McNally. The final hopes rested with Jacobson. He sent a roller to Scott at shortstop and then, to the amazement of all, stopped halfway to first and watched as Pipp made the put-out. If Pipp had dropped the ball he would still have been able to make the play. But why, as the *Post-Dispatch* put it, "with a pennant and $4500 [World Series money] at stake," did Jacobson not run out the play? Ruth, who had a daily ghostwritten column at this time, came down hard on "Jake." He cited the incident as proof that the Browns knew they were beaten. Johnny Tobin had perhaps the best explanation when he indicated that the Browns' center fielder had wrenched his knee fielding Witt's single and had further strained it batting.

"It would not have been so bad," said one fan to the *Post-Dispatch*, "if the Yanks had walloped their way to a one side victory. But for the Browns to be virtually in first place and then kick it away, that was a heartbreaker."

"And last evening the townspeople mourned," added the *Post-Dispatch.*

Fohl's moves concerning the removal of Davis received the most attention in the post mortem department. He explained them to the *Post-Dispatch*:

> When a passed ball put Schang on second with no outs, and Elmer Smith, a good left hand hitter, batting, I believed that Davis, a right hand pitcher, should be relieved. Smith is a dangerous hitter; more dangerous than any other pinch hitter New York has. I wanted Smith out of there and I knew if I switched to Pruett he would be replaced.
>
> Smith was taken out and then McNally replaced him. McNally was not up there to hit. He was up there to sacrifice. Our play was to catch Schang at third. McNally bunted and if Hank Severeid had handled his bunt as Hank handles 99% out of 100 such bunts, Schang would have been out at third and I believe we would have been out of the hole.
>
> Had Schang been caught at third, it would have left a man on first base with one out and Scott and Bush coming up. Either Pruett or Shocker would have cleaned that situation up in a hurry, I believe. But my principal object in sending Pruett in at the time I did was to get Elmer Smith out of there. It was just an unfortunate break that it did not work out.
>
> The Browns feel the sting of that defeat, of course, but we are not out of the pennant race. We still have a chance and we'll be in there fighting today and tomorrow and for the rest of the season. New York can not afford to take us lightly. They were lucky to leave St. Louis in first place.

Many, of course, disagreed with Fohl's reasoning feeling that Davis had pitched well and should have been allowed to remain in the game. Among those with that opinion was Ruth. In his ghosted column he said:

> Instead of allowing Davis to work out his own salvation, Manager Lee Fohl of the Browns sent Pruett, a little left hander to his relief. . . . Pruett then . . . was in turn replaced on the hill by Urban Shocker. If Fohl had any intention of

> using Shocker in this game he should have sent him in when Davis was withdrawn. In my opinion Fohl made one mistake in pulling Davis, and another when he sent Pruett instead of Shocker to his rescue.

Befitting the occasion, L. C. Davis lamented in "The Pennant Blues":

Oh, sad are the hearts of the St. Louis rooters.
And silent and hushed are the zippy horn-tooters
The hearts of the fans to the innermost cockle
Are withered and seared by that Yankee debacle
The heads of our heroes in sadness are bowed–
Oh, why should the spirit of mortal be proud?

They gallantly fought to the very last inning
And up to the ninth were undoubtedly winning
The fans were prepared from the field to escort 'em
But sadly retired to hold a post-mortem
And over the city there hovers a cloud–
Oh, why should the spirit of mortal be proud?

There's many a slip 'twixt the lip and the flagon
Just when we're preparing to mount the band wagon
The fortunes of baseball are very uncertain
So on the sad scene let us lower the curtain
Instead of a pennant we'll order a shroud
Oh, why should the spirit of mortal be proud?

Virtually lost in the agony of defeat was the final outcome of the bottle throwing incident. On Monday, September 18, there were accounts that deputy federal district court clerk Joseph Walsh had seen a ten-year-old boy throw the bottle and run toward the nearest exit. Walsh was among those on the field and felt that the boy could not have seen Witt. He thought it was possible he was trying to hit the ball. In any event the youngster escaped in the excitement of the moment.

Joining Phil Ball in offering a reward for the apprehension of the bottle thrower were American League president Ban

Johnson with $1,000, the St. Louis Cardinals with $500, and the Booster's Club with $50, for a total of $2,050.

The *Post-Dispatch* commented editorially after the series that St. Louis fandom could take solace in the fact that the age of the alleged thrower and his apparent lack of malicious intent coupled with the remorse expressed on Saturday at the park was sufficient pennance. As incredible as it may seem, the ultimate determination was that Witt stepped on a bottle already on the field, causing it to fly up and hit him in the head! If that seems a bit farfetched then consider that the originator of this theory, St. Louis salesman James Hon, was presented with a World Series ticket, rail transportation to the series, and $100 by Ban Johnson.

The Browns were still only a game and a half back with nine left to play. The sixth-place Senators were due in for three games starting on Tuesday, September 19, and they were to be followed by the even lowlier Philadelphia Athletics for three more. The season would end with three games against the first division contending Chicago White Sox. The Yankees would conclude their season with three games each with Detroit, Cleveland, Boston, and a single game with Washington. All of these games would be played on the road. Despite the apparent schedule advantage of the Browns, St. Louis partisans were quick to point out that clubs coming into Sportsman's Park would have their best pitchers available. Washington had Walter Johnson, George Mogridge, and Tom Zachary; Philadelphia had 26-game winner Ed Rommel; Chicago had Urban Faber, Charley Robertson, "Dixie" Leverett, and Ted Blankenship. Meanwhile New York would face their only really tough pitching in Detroit against Herman Pillette, "Red" Oldham, and Howard Ehmke. However, despite the weak pitching in Boston, the Red Sox were the only team to have a season's edge on the Yankees, and they would surely face a tough pitcher in the final game at Washington.

That tough pitcher was Walter Johnson, and it was he who opened the first game against the Browns. Mirroring the feelings of the crowd of 3,000 to 4,000, the weather was dark and cloudy and rain fell during part of the game. But the spirits of the players were high despite the weather and the events of the previous day. Pat Collins played for Sisler at first base and homered in the seventh to give the club a 2–1 lead. Williams had earlier hit his thirty-ninth, which would be his last, but enough to win the league home run title. But the Senators got to Vangilder in the eighth for three runs and a 4–2 lead.

Prior to the Yankee series the Browns routinely pulled off late-inning rallies to win games. It almost happened this time, and Pat Collins would have been the hero. In the ninth, with Severeid on first, Collins sent a drive to center which hit the bleacher screen a foot or so below the top. It went for a double, scoring Severeid, rather than another home run and a tie game. Collins died at second and Washington won 4–3. New York was beating Detroit and the Browns were now two and a half back. Sisler did pinch-hit in the eigth, but his swing was stiff and he struck out.

Despite still being relatively close in the race it appeared as if St. Louis was more than willing to write off the team. *Post-Dispatch* sports editor John Wray conceded that a mathematical possibility still existed, but concluded:

> The Browns now must face one or two pitchers who are almost certain to beat them; while they must themselves rely upon hurlers concerning whose efficiency no man can predict.
>
> A miracle of a railroad wreck might put them across as flag winners this year.
>
> However, they seem to have missed their best chance in 34 years through the hardest of hard fortune and are more to be pitied than censured....

A mere 2,000 turned out for the second Washington game as Fohl sent Shocker out to try to keep the team close. Shocker was pounded for 15 hits, the Browns got only four, and Washington won its second in a row, 5–0. J. Roy Stockton covered that game for the *Post-Dispatch*, and the tone of his writing as well as the incident he describes reflect the despair of those days following the Yankee series:

> Suddenly there came a raucous jeer from the upper deck of the grandstand.
>
> "Hurrah for Shocker," jeered the disguntled fan, and in the silence of the game, a game being played because the schedule demands that each team play 154 games, that jeer could be heard from one end of Sportsman's Park to the other.
>
> "Hurrah for Shocker, Blah! Blah! Blah!" An ironic laugh punctuated the jeer.
>
> Shocker . . . stepped back from the slab from which he was about to deliver a pitch and he focused his eyes on the disgruntled fan. There was no chance of making a mistake. There was a fan here and a fan there and in between hundreds of empty seats sticking out like the ribs on a skeleton, the skeleton of the once very plump and very active pennant chance.
>
> Shocker looked at his tormentor for a moment and then finished the inning. When he walked to the bench several men sitting behind the dugout leaned over and spoke to Shocker. Then those men hurredly left their seats.
>
> At the same time the fan in the upper grandstand left his seat. At first he walked slowly. Then he broke into a frightened rush. Then he reached down and picked up a pop bottle and held it in his hand as one would hold a rock or billy.
>
> When the fan reached the top of the stairway leading from the stand he met the men who had been sitting behind the Browns' dugout. They were friends of Shocker. The fan trembled, shook from head to foot, turned pale, pleaded that he had bet some money on the game and might be excused for hooting a bit at Shocker.
>
> When the poor, trembling lout was about to be slammed on the ear several police stepped in. They led him away, white and trembling. Down to the exit he went and when he was safely outside the gate he broke into a frantic run. He caught a Natural Bridge car (trolley) going north on Spring Avenue and his fear inspired such speed and nimbleness that he did not wait for the car to stop, but leaped with ape like agility onto the bumper on the rear of the car and pulled himself into the car through the platform window.

Wray, who had himself written off the team the prior day, now sanctimoniously proclaimed:

> The Great St. Louis Pennant Bubble having been punctured, the Mound City fans have quit the team almost unanimously....
>
> In short, the fans have folded up on the club, notwithstanding one of the most gallant fights ever made by a pennant candidate. The Browns certainly deserve better than to play out their season's string before empty seats.

Years later Bill Jacobson would comment to the *Sporting News* about the first two games of the Washington series:

> I also blame our club for not hustling more after the Yankees beat us, two out of three, in a September series. After the Yanks left town, we blew our next games to Washington, then a second division club. When we eventually lost the pennant only by a game, the importance of those Washington defeats may well be realized.

Jacobson certainly hustled himself in the last game of the Washington series as he paced the team with a home run, triple, and two singles in five at-bats. Fohl had started the little-used Bill Bayne, and the team had come-up with seven runs going into the seventh. Washington came alive for five runs and Pruett was sent in to stem the tide. The Senators came up with another run in the ninth, but the Browns were able to hang on for the 7–6 win. It did them no good in the standings as the Yankees maintained their three-and-a-half game lead by continuing to master Detroit. Sisler continued on the bench, and Fohl gave Josh Billings his only start of the year behind the plate. Fewer than 2,000 turned out for the game.

Despite the victory the crowd was about the same on September 22 for the first game of the Philadelphia series. But there was a difference. Sisler was back on first base, and he was also the reigning Most Valuable Player in the American League. The league had revived the award in 1922 after a long lapse and placed the selection procedures in the hands of an eight-man sports editor committee chaired by Mr. I. E. Sanborn. The eight represented each league city with St. Louis being represented by *Post-Dispatch* sports editor John Wray. The members voted for eight players of their choice with number one getting eight votes, number two seven, etc. Sisler got a total of 50 votes while Philadelphia pitcher Ed Rommel came in second with 31. It was originally the league's intention to erect a $100,000 monument in Washington on which would annually be engraved each season's winner. That plan never was realized, but the National League soon joined the voting practice, which continues to this day. At about the same time Sisler and Shocker were named to Babe Ruth's All American baseball team, which was featured in Ruth's newspaper column.

With Sisler back at first base, Fohl returned Ellerbe to third and sent Collins behind the plate. The changes seemed to work wonders as the team responded with one of their classic hitting attacks, collecting fifteen hits off two Philadelphia pitchers for an 11–5 win. Ray Kolp went all the way for the complete game victory, while Sisler got one hit in five tries. While the results buoyed the sagging spirits, the Yankees continued to win, this time at Cleveland, and their lead held.

The brief two-game winning streak came to an end the following day as Philadelphia built a 6–2 lead over the first seven innings. The Browns came back to make it close, but fell short 6–5. Vangilder was ineffective over the first three innings and was relieved by Pruett, who did bring some cheers by striking out the side in the seventh. Fohl continued the same lineup and Sisler again went one for five. Meanwhile in Cleveland the Yankees increased their lead to four and one-half games, virtually assuring them the flag. The Browns would now have to win all their four remaining games while New York dropped their last five in order to gain a tie. A remote possibility, but it almost happened!

On Sunday, September 24, "Dixie" Davis made his first start since the epic Monday game, and George Sisler regained his old form in dramatic fashion. Davis needed help from Wright in the sixth when the Athletics drew close at 5–4, but Wright one-hit them the rest of the way. Sisler got three singles, scored three runs, and stole two bases as the Browns went on to win 7–4. Cleveland stopped the New York pennant march and the lead was reduced to three and one-half games. The 7,500 that turned out for the game was in sharp contrast to most recent crowds, but they were no doubt more encouraged with Sisler's performance as it might relate to the future than with any remote pennant chances remaining.

Still the chances were there. The schedule now had the Browns off until Friday, September 29 – an unusual four-day break that had not previously occurred in the season. The Yankees had a similar break, but not quite as long. They were due to play in Boston on September 28, 29, and 30 before going to Washington to end the season on October 1. The Browns would close the season with three games against the White Sox on September 29, 30, and October 1. New York gave those chances some hope by losing the first two games in Boston. Including the last game in Cleveland, the Yankees had now lost three in a row while scoring only one run and getting 14 hits in those games. The losing pitchers in the contests had been aces Bob Shawkey and Joe Bush.

Perhaps New York could still be had. Adding encouragement to those hopes was an announcement from the American League office in Chicago that if the race did wind up in a tie there would be a five-game playoff. The first two games would be held in St. Louis on Tuesday, October 3, and Wednesday, October 4. The scene would shift to New York on Thursday, October 6, and if necessary, Friday, October 7. Should the series be tied the site of the deciding fifth game would be determined by a coin toss. The latter seems today a strange way of coming up with a playoff site. It would appear New York should have been awarded the site based on their dominance of the season series, 14 games to 8.

Even further encouragement was fueled when Johnny Tobin drove two bases-empty home runs into the stands to help defeat

Chicago 3–2 in the first game of the closing series. Vangilder gave the White Sox only five hits as the Browns beat Chicago's best pitcher, Urban Faber. The Yankee lead was now two games, and both fans and ownership in the "Checkbook Capital," as the St. Louis press liked to refer to New York, were getting uneasy.

"I have no doubt that he Yankees will win," the *New York Times* quoted a Yankee fan, "but I wish they would hurry up with the job." *Post-Dispatch* sports editor John Wray covered the Friday game himself and gleefully commented: "If the despised discards [Boston Red Sox, many of whom were ex–Yankees] should knock his [Yankee owner Jacob Ruppert] team out of a pennant he would require an asbestos muffler about the region of his verbal exhaust." Boston would prove to be the one team to take the season series from New York despite a last-place finish.

It was of course not to be. Boston manager Hugh Duffy started Alex Ferguson, to the surprise of many who thought he would go with Herb Pennock in the Saturday, September 30, game. The Yankees wasted no time in getting to Ferguson. Witt led off with a single past Red Sox second baseman Del Pratt. Dugan got another to short right. This brought up Ruth with instructions to bunt. When future Brown Frank O'Rourke slipped in fielding the ball the bases were loaded. Pipp then singled to right, scoring Witt and Dugan and sending Ferguson to the showers. Now Duffy brought in Pennock, and while Meusel's sacrifice fly would score another run, the crafty Pennock allowed only two more hits and shut out New York the rest of the way. Needless to say there was much speculation in St. Louis concerning Boston's failure to start Pennock in the first place. As it was the Yankees needed no further runs as starter Waite Hoyt was relieved by Bush to retire the side for the victory and pennant.

The Browns' game with the White Sox in St. Louis was in the fifth inning when the score of the New York-Boston game was posted. The Browns had built up a lopsided 9–1 lead by that time as Urban Shocker sought to keep them in the race. The day had been designated in his honor, and prior to the game the 8,000 fans saw the Browns' "meal ticket" presented with a seven-passenger touring car. Fohl had started the identical lineup with which he had started the season against this same Chicago team. Ellerbe was at third base and Severeid was back behind the plate. However, once the score was posted there was a noticeable letup on the field. Shocker had given the White Sox only five hits to that point, but over the last four innings he was hit eight times for six runs. Both McManus and Ellerbe made costly errors to contribute to the Chicago rally. Nonetheless it was an 11–7 victory with George Sisler once again looking his old self with a single, double, and home run.

There remained but the formality of playing out the scheduled Sunday game on October 1. Fohl let some of the reserves play and gave the start to Bayne. Gene Robertson, who would eventually become the club's regular third baseman, relieved Gerber at short, Durst took over from Jacobson in center, and Pat Collins caught for Severeid. While it meant nothing, the surprising crowd of 7,500 was treated to an excellent game. The Browns were the victims of a triple play for the fourth time in the season in the second inning. With Durst on second and McManus at first, Pat Collins lined to Chicago Hall of Fame second baseman Eddie Collins. Collins stepped on the bag for the second out and threw to first before McManus could get back. Chicago led 1–0 going into the seventh before McManus tripled in Durst with the tying run. The Browns went out in style, with the winning run coming across in the bottom of the ninth and one of the reserves the hero. Williams, who would have liked to have hit his fortieth homer, instead had to settle for a walk. Durst sacrificed him to second, but McManus then grounded to Chicago shortstop Ernie Johnson, who threw late to third attempting to get Williams. Chicago pitcher "Dixie" Leverett then struck out Pat Collins for the second out. Then Gene Robertson, who was batting for only the twenty-seventh time that season, lined to right, scoring Williams for the Browns' ninety-third victory. The Yankees didn't have to win at Washington – and didn't. The final standings read:

	Won	Lost	Pct.
New York	94	60	.610
St. Louis	93	61	.604

Most of the players departed on Monday, October 2, for their homes, though some left after the final game. George Sisler headed up a group of major league barnstormers that was to tour New England starting on Tuesday. Sisler was accompanied as far as Cleveland on his trip east by Lee Fohl, who made his home there. "Chick" Shorten was the only Brown to play with Sisler, while Ken Williams declined an opportunity to play for expenses only on a Japanese tour.

The Browns' failure to win the pennant with what was without a doubt their finest team has been hashed over by baseball men through the years. Frank Ellerbe would cite the lack of reserve strength as a reason, while others would simply recite the long list of misfortunes which seemed to plague the team through the season: Shocker's nearly three-week absence from the rotation in June and early July; having to play three nearly consecutive doubleheaders in Boston before coming to New York in early July; the two "Eddie Foster" incidents; Sisler's injury just before the "Little World Series"; Schang's single off Davis' glove in the disastrous game followed by Severeid's bad throw attempting to get Schang; and finally, Boston's failure to start Herb Pennock against the Yankees on September 30.

The author believes the answer lies in an L. C. Davis poem, "Next Year":

Oh somewhere in this favored land
  The people shout and laugh
And we will join 'em when we land
  A first class pitching staff

Our Brownies can field and slug
  Are game as fighting cocks
They'll win the pennant when they plug
  That leaky pitching box

They battled to the final ditch
  And set the fans aflame
But lacked the hurlers who could pitch
  A full nine inning game

Although beneath the strain they broke
  Just take a tip from me
And keep your eye upon their smoke
  In nineteen twenty three.

8

AFTERMATH

Last Days and Last Hurrahs

The Yankees went on to oppose their co-tenant and landlord of the Polo Grounds, the Giants, in the second of what would be three consecutive "Subway Series." It would be the last staged exclusively in the Polo Grounds as the Yankees would begin play the following season in their new facility across the Harlem River, Yankee Stadium.

The Giants were to insure that the Yankees' last days at the Polo Grounds were not very pleasant. The American League champions had closed their schedule by losing four of their last five games. They proceeded to lose four more to the Giants, their best effort being the only tie game in World Series history, 3–3 in the ten-inning second game. The scores were relatively close, 3–2, 3–0, 4–3, and 5–3, but the Yankee offense was virtually nonexistent. The Giant pitchers held Ruth to a .118 average (2 for 17) and the team to .203. Only Pipp (.286) and Meusel (.300) hit for a respectable average among the regulars. In game three, Giants hurler Jack Scott gave up only four hits, while fellow pitcher Art Nehf surrendered only five in the 5–3 clincher. Meanwhile, neither Bush, Hoyt, nor Mays could contain the Giants, who were paced by third baseman Heine Groh (.474) and Hall of Fame second baseman Frank Fisch (.471).

Bill Jacobson would later tell the *Sporting News*:

> That Yankee team of 1922, the one which beat us out by a game, didn't win a game from the Giants in the World Series of that year. The best they got was a ten inning tie. I don't know whether we could have beaten McGraw's 1922 team, but I'll bet my life we could have made a better Series showing than did those Yankees.

Nonetheless, the Yankees did collect $3,225.00 apiece in World Series receipts as American League champions. The Browns, as the second-place team, divided up a pot of $18,548.23, which came out to 28 shares worth $662.44 each. Additionally, Frederick Lieb indicated Ball gave the players another $20,000 to split among themselves. Bob Quinn also received a bonus while Shocker had previously been give $5,000 in mid-season. While it is an admitted cliche to say that 1922 dollars were worth more than the current variety it is nonetheless true. Dollars were something that players of that era, with a few obvious exceptions such as Ruth, did not see a great deal of. Frank Ellerbe recalled the salary situation; he himself was paid $4,500, but had no idea what his teammates received:

> I don't know what they were paying [Shocker] then.... Nobody knew what they [others] were getting. I imagine the top of what any one of them were paying. Connie Mack wasn't paying anything. Griff [Washington owner Clark Griffith] wasn't and the Browns couldn't. . . . $5 or $10,000, $10,000 maybe, something like that. . . . George Sisler, he was the highest paid player on the team and I don't imagine he got more than 15, maybe 20, if that much. Nobody talked salaries at all....

Dorothy Brady added concerning her father, John Tobin:

> I would say, if I can remember my mother saying something about that, between $10 and $12,000 a year. Something like that. . . . Of course at that time that was not considered too bad. . . . In those days they lived fairly well on that.

Contract negotiations were sometimes conducted at the end of the season rather than through the mail in the December-January time period. Washington followed that practice, and Frank Ellerbe remembers his discussions with Clark Griffith:

> Griff wanted to sign me after 1919 for the coming season of '20. Griff was pretty hard to deal with then. . . . He got a lot of those Cuban players for practically nothing, $150 or $200. . . . He wanted to sign me after the 1919 season was over. He called me over to the office. That was a habit, tried to sign all the players before they left. He wanted to sign me for $2,500. "No, no. I don't have to play baseball for a living. My father left farm lands and all. I just came up to see if I could play major league baseball." Anyway he asked me what I would sign for and I told him, well I'd sign for $3,500. "Whoa," he says. "Joe Dugan, the best third baseman in the league playing for Connie Mack (at that time), is not getting that much." "I don't have a thing to do with what Joe Dugan gets. I know what I'd play for." . . . Before we were leaving that fall Sam Agnew told me confidentially: "Old Griff's going to sign you pretty quick now, call you up to the office, make him pay you. . . . He hasn't got any infielders, infielders are hard to get now." I told Griff I'd pack up and quit baseball . . . so he gave me the $3,500 I asked for.

Money may not have been available in great quantities for the Browns, but the message that seems to run through my research is that they played for the sheer pleasure of it. While the pay for most may not have been equal to their talents, this disparity seems not to have left any traces of bitterness. They seem as a group to have been – much more than their counterparts in New York – classic "nice guys." Jim Tobin remembered:

> These players were more team players at that time, even the stars like George Sisler, he was just like anybody else. . . . I do remember one thing that happened to Ken Williams in one of those games toward the end of the season. He hit one ball that bounced over . . . off the ground over the wire fence in right field. Happened to be a friend of mine that

caught the ball. It was over the wire which went for a home run and the kid came back and I said: "Well come on. I'll take you upstairs [to the club house]." And he got an extra ball from Ken Williams for catching that.

Frank Ellerbe:

We were playing in Washington. . . . [A former instructor] Professor Norts came out to see me. . . . We were all around the lobby of the hotel out there. . . . It rained out or something. We were all sitting around in there. I introduced Professor Norts. He was a great baseball fan. When I was playing at Sewanee [University of the South] he came out to see me. I took him around and introduced him to the boys [Browns] and all. Before he left he says: "That's the finest bunch of fellows I ever saw." The best behaved crowd of young men he ever saw. He was impressed. They all worked together . . . a good ball club.

And what would be the normal road routine of these men? Morning practice, even on game days, was quite common. A light lunch would be served at the hotel at noon and then it would be off to the park for the game. At this time single games would normally start at 3:00 or 3:30 p.m. and rarely took longer than two hours. Then the team returned to the hotel for dinner. The evenings were spent in the hotel lobby, smoking; at the silent movies of the day; or in various rooms playing cards. Both Frank Ellerbe and Jim Tobin have alluded to a certain amount of "running around," which certainly could be expected among any traveling group of men. However, there can be little doubt that these players lived the game much more than the contemporary variety. The lobby-sitting involved much shop talk and study of the daily newspapers to see what was happening around the league.

When the American League released its pitching statistics in early December 1922 they revealed to the surprise of many that the St. Louis staff had the best earned run average in the league. The Browns staff came in a 3.33 to New York's 3.42 – despite the fact that the Yankee staff led in complete games, 98 to 79, and that they were always conceded to have the finest array of starters in the league with Bush, Shawkey, Hoyt, and Mays.

The Browns continued to make efforts to improve their pitching, but no deal could be worked out to the satisfaction of Fohl, Quinn, or Ball. That situation prompted one New York writer to predict that the club would finish fifth in 1923. While that proved to be a most accurate prophecy, the main reason was to be other than pitching.

As the year turned there were reports of Sisler's continuing problem with his shoulder. He continued to be treated by Dr. Hyland, but complained of a slight kink. Despite the injury, it will be recalled, Sisler had returned to the lineup for the last six games of the season and then gone on a barnstorming tour. The situation was of obvious concern to the Browns management, but there were always assurances that the American League's Most Valuable Player would be ready for the start of the season. However, there were press reports that the club would be looking into a back-up first baseman for the first time in years.

By late January Davis, Ellerbe, Ezzell (rookie), and Billings had signed their contracts. There was speculation that Ken Williams might be difficult to sign after his brilliant 1922 season, but this was quickly dispelled when he wrote Bob Quinn that he was anxious to start the season and expected to knock in another 20 runs above his 1922 figure of 155. By mid–February most of the big names had mailed in their contracts: Kolp, Wright, Foster, Austin, Gerber, Jacobson, and Shocker. The remainder would soon follow, and the team once again assembled at Mobile for spring training. Sisler was not among those making the trip to Alabama, though by early February both the Browns' first baseman and Dr. Hyland were indicating that the shoulder was showing steady improvement. Hyland insinuated that Sisler would have no problem with it for the coming season.

Spring training opened, and by March 10 the Browns were ready to play their first exhibition game against Mobile. But there was still no Sisler. His absence was viewed as ominous by the team. If the shoulder had not responded to treatment over the off-season, the players reasoned, then what difference would another week make? Ken Williams summarized it best when he told the *Post-Dispatch*'s J. Roy Stockton: "If Sisler can't play we're ruined. We can fill any other gaps that exist, but there's no other Sisler."

Quinn arrived in Mobile to see the Browns start the exhibition season and sought to dispel the gloom. He for the first time brought a new aspect of Sisler's problem into focus. It was not the shoulder injury that was keeping George in St. Louis; it was the recovery period from an attack of influenza. Why should he come to spring training while still weak? Someone like Sisler would only need a week to get into condition anyway. Quinn concluded to Stockton with words he would soon eat: "There is no danger that he will be unable to start the season." Still the speculation among the players continued. Quinn called the team together on March 14 to explain about the influenza attack and answer queries as to why "Stuffy" McInnis had not been signed as insurance. McInnis had been released by Cleveland after the 1922 season and was available in early March. Quinn, perhaps revealing the true depth of the Sisler problem, indicated the Browns tried to sign McInnis, but his wife preferred that he join the Boston Braves so that the family could remain in that city.

Two days later the story broke in St. Louis that there was a real possibility that Sisler would not only miss spring training, but opening day as well. It was revealed that the Browns' mainstay was threatened with a nasal operation to relieve sinus trouble which had bothered him since his recovery from the influenza attack. An operation would be necessary if the nasal obstruction did not respond to treatment. Sisler told the *Post-Dispatch*'s Joseph Holland:

> I have not advised Quinn or Fohl about this condition because I have always believed that I would be ready to play at the opening of the season. I have not yet resigned myself to a late start, but I'll need at least two weeks' training to time a ball properly in hitting. I am in good physical condition

> [otherwise], but it would be useless to go to camp at this time because it would only aggravate this condition and make matters worse.

There appeared to be no further concern about the right shoulder, which was reportedly as strong as ever though not yet tested.

Back in Mobile Fohl had used McManus at first, but soon switched to rookie Harry Rice, who had minor league experience at the position. The team was now preparing to wrap up their series of initial exhibitions with Mobile and move into Texas League country for further competition. Over the next two and a half weeks exhibition series would be played against Shreveport, Dallas, Wichita Falls, and Fort Worth of the Texas League. The Browns would then play two games at New Orleans against Columbus (American Association) and three against New Orleans (Southern Association). From there the team would head back to St. Louis with a two-game stop against Memphis (Southern Association) before returning home for the now two-game city series with the Cardinals.

During the trip into Texas Fohl decided to try Cedric Durst at first base and Gene Robertson at third. Both were starting their second season with the Browns after seeing relatively little service in 1922. Robertson would ultimately share the third base job with rookie Homer Ezzel; this, along with Dave Danforth's full-time return to the club, would be the only signficant change in the Browns' lineup, other than first base, from 1922.

Despite the earlier report that Sisler might miss opening day, he had remained optimistic that that would not occur. He had made tentative plans to join the team at Shreveport on April 2. Then on March 27 it was announced that while the sinus condition was yielding to treatment, the progress as such was not rapid enough to allow the trip. For the first time reference was made to a "slight muscular eye disturbance." Assurances were given – apparently to contradict speculation that Sisler's eyesight was impaired – that this was not of any consequence as to cause any playing inconvenience.

As in the prior year John Tobin, Hank Severeid, and Ken Williams were able to leave the team early to return to St. Louis. Tobin attempted to make the best front possible on the Sisler problem when he told the *Post-Dispatch*'s Joseph Holland on April 7:

> The club has not allowed itself to be fooled by false hopes. No one has the idea that George will play opening day. But we do believe that we can put a strong team in the field without Sisler. We'll stay up there until George gets back and then the added strength he gives us will carry us away ahead. Oh, we've got it all figured out.
>
> . . . The team is far from being a dead one. Fans through the South, who had seen both our club and the Yanks, said we were far ahead of them in pep and fight.

Sisler himself downplayed his absence, citing all the other .300 hitters on the club, but adding rather weakly: ". . . and the pitchers look pretty good."

Then on April 11 came the front-page blockbuster. Sisler would be operated on for the relief of the sinus condition on April 13 and would have to sit out until at least June 1. It was now openly revealed that the condition had in fact resulted in an impairment of Sisler's vision. Once the operation was complete his treatment would be in the hands of an eye specialist. The sinus operation was a necessary step before the treatment of the eyes could be brought to a successful conclusion. In most professions one could expect to lose only about ten days of normal activity. The fact that Sisler was an athlete extended this time extensively. It was pointed out that breathing the dust on the diamond could aggravate an unhealed wound.

And so the team which had gone down to the wire with the Yankees the year before was faced with playing at least the first third of the season without the player who was regarded as the finest in the game at that time. The brave fronts continued. Said the *Post-Dispatch*'s J. Roy Stockton on the eve of the city series:

> In fact, the more you analyze the Browns' resources the less excuses you find for singing the second division blues. There are too many stars on the roster, too much strength, to count the team out. If it gets off to a fair start and Cedric Durst is patient and not worried over any mistakes he may happen to make, the Browns will be hard to best.

Sisler himself issued this statement just after the city series:

> I was delighted at the wonderful showing of the club on Saturday and Sunday. It shows certainly, that we have a real ball club, a well balanced team.
>
> I feel sure that it [his absence] will not make a great difference. At the earliest possible moment, just as soon as I am able to do, I will give what assistance I can to Durst, if he doesn't mind. And I'm sure he won't for he's a very fine fellow.
>
> All that I can say now is that I am very hopeful.

Certainly the Browns had cause for some optimism after the Cardinal games. On April 14 Vangilder and Shocker combined for a five-hitter as Robertson got a home run in the 3–0 victory. The following day the results were even better. Pruett went the distance, giving the Cardinals only six hits, while the Browns pounded out 16 in the 11–3 romp. Adding to the joy was a home run by the Sisler heir apparent, Cedric Durst, as well as one by Williams.

But once the season got underway it was evident that the loss of Sisler was taking its toll. The Browns were in seventh place on April 28 and rose only to sixth on May 12, shortly before the Yankees paid their first visit of the year. Durst had soon gotten into Fohl's doghouse by his failure to hit, and McManus was moved to first base. The veteran Eddie Foster, normally a third baseman, took over at second. But that didn't work either. Foster hit no better than Durst, and it seemed clear that he was now past the age of being able to play every day.

Finally on May 16 after having dropped three straight to New York, Quinn was able to solve the problem to some degree. Fred

"Dutch" Schliebner, who had finished second in the Southern Association batting race in 1922 with a .354 average, was obtained from Brooklyn of the National League. The Browns gave up another "Dutch," Frank Henry, a pitcher who had been with the team briefly in 1922. Schliebner had become expendable to Brooklyn when Jack Fournier had been signed. Most observers felt he was an adequate fielder, but had reservations about his ability to hit major league pitching. While certainly there could be no one who would adequately replace Sisler, Schliebner would prove to be a competent journeyman who would hit .271 and then disappear from the major leagues forever after this lone season.

Schliebner's arrival produced no miracles, and the team stayed largely in fifth and sixth place, with a brief excursion to fourth, until mid–July. It had now become clearly apparent that Sisler's return in 1923 was highly doubtful. But the rumor mill was turning rapidly, and there were press reports on July 9 that he would replace Fohl as manager after the season, health permitting. The reports went further than that in indicating Phil Ball's increasing displeasure with Fohl's handling of the team and suggesting that the St. Louis owner was looking for an immediate temporary replacement until Sisler could take command. Ball denied the reports and Fohl, typically, would not comment.

Suddenly the team began to play well. By July 15 they were in third place and were still there at the end of the month with a 49-44 record. They trailed second-place Cleveland by only five games. There was increased speculation that Sisler might in fact be able to play before the end of the season. There were those who pointed to the fact that Sisler had worn glasses when he attended the first game of the Yankee series in mid–May, but had not done so for a like game in early July. Those who saw him play golf could not detect that he had any vision problem.

But on August 1 Sisler was forgotten as the Danforth problem reared its ugly head for the second and final time. The Browns were playing a doubleheader in Philadelphia against the Athletics. Danforth was working the first game when umpire George Moriarity ejected the lefthander for alleged discoloration of the ball. The ejection carried with it an automatic ten-day suspension and brought a flurry of protests from the Browns—that is, all except Fohl. The players drew up a telegram of protest to send to American League president Ban Johnson, but the manager refused to sign it, and the idea was discarded. Ray Gillespie provided some insight into Fohl's thinking and the feelings of the team:

> Fohl always had the feeling that Danforth was a cheater and the rest of the players took Dave at his word that he wasn't. Nobody ever proved it. Danforth down through the years, we became very close friends . . . always explained to me that he did nothing wrong. Absolutely no cheating. He never admitted to anybody that he cheated. . . . The players resented Fohl's attitude toward him. The whole thing just blew up. They made Jimmy Austin the manager.

Fohl's position had simply now become untenable. His refusal to support Danforth left him with a disgruntled and unhappy team. He would make no comment on Danforth other than to say that his suspension would hurt the team. Things deteriorated further two days later in Boston when Fohl gave the wrong batting order to the umpire. One batter was declared out in the first inning and another in the ninth for not following the order given the umpire. That incident, coupled with Fohl's failure to bait the umpire in a dispute which resulted in the ejection of Tobin and Shocker, only made the situation worse.

The axe fell on August 7 when Ball wired Fohl as reported in the *Post-Dispatch*:

> For the good of the game and morale of the players you are hereby immediately relieved from management of the team. I have wired Mr. Friel [business manager Bill Friel had succeeded Bob Quinn when the latter left to become part of the new ownership group of the Boston Red Sox] to appoint a new manager.
>
> Fohl was disturbed at the wording "good of the game" and later got Ball to amend that to read: "good of the game

as played by the Browns and for the morale of the Browns' team." While he would comment no further it was reported that he was privately pleased with the action, which removed the burden of an unhappy team from his shoulders. He was on hand as a spectator when Austin took over on August 8 and led the club to a now rare 4–3 win over the New York Yankees.

Austin kept the team in either third or fourth place until the final week of the season, when a disastrous 1-6 week dropped them into fifth, where they would finish. Could the absence of one man, albeit a superstar, make essentially the same team a second-division finisher? Ray Gillespie answered affirmatively: "They missed 'Sis,' they missed Sisler tremendously. He just carried that team in '22. All the others, the hitting of Tobin and Williams, 'Jake' and all just meshed in. 'Sis' was the big cog in that machine. Without him they were nothing."

In late September just prior to the end of the regular season it was reported that Sisler would be able to play in 1924. Sometime thereafter he was named playing manager. His tenure would last three years and include a fourth-place finish in 1924 with the identical 74-78 record of the prior year; a third place finish in 1925, which meant a share of the World Series money; and a disastrous seventh place finish in 1926. He gave up managing after that season, which had seen him drop to a .289 average, and was strictly a player in 1927. Phil Ball cleaned out the last of the old crew after that season, and Sisler found himself with Washington at the beginning of the following season. It would be a short stay. After a poor start he was waived out of the American League to the Boston Braves. While he could still hit .300 – he did so for his three year stay with the Braves – it was evident that his legs were gone. By 1931 he was in the minors with Rochester of the International League. He of course hit over .300 on a team that won the league title and the right to oppose the American Association's St. Paul Saints in the Junior World Series.

Thus one of the game's greatest stars who was denied the opportunity to play in the "big" World Series would now have a chance to play in at least the next best thing. But fate was to play a cruel role. The series opened in St. Paul on October 1, and Sisler came to bat for the first time in the second inning. He lined a single to center and as he ran to first he pulled a groin muscle. A pinch-runner was sent in for him, and he never appeared in another game. Rochester ultimately won the best-of-nine series five games to three, but Sisler would play no significant role in that victory. After spending the 1932 season as player-manager with Tyler of the Texas League, he retired from the game.

Sisler would spend most of the 1930s in the printing and sporting goods businesses, operating ball parks for night softball, and supervising a national semi-pro baseball tournament. When the Baseball Hall of Fame opened in 1939 he had already been voted in among the first fifteen players so honored. His old friend Branch Rickey brought him back to the majors as a special instructor and scout. When Rickey moved on to Pittsburgh in 1951, Sisler went with him. He passed away in St. Louis on March 26, 1973, at the age of 80. He was undoubtedly the greatest Brown of them all and one of the game's all-time greats. Ray Gillespie explained his charisma:

> Everybody on the ball club sort of looked up to him as their leader. Like little boy blue, could do no wrong. "Sis," that was the nickname, that was how they referred to him. I think they regarded him with reverance, kindness. . . . He was so good, exceptional that year. Everybody knew how hard he was trying, all the heroics and things. . . . Likeable? Yes. Very much so. He was a shy person, wasn't a pushy type. Very shy. Generally spoke when he was spoken to. Had very little to say. Bashful. Actually bashful. That's the kind of person he was.

The first of the 1922 team to die was Urban Shocker at the age of 38 on September 9, 1928. The one-man pitching staff pitched again for the Browns in 1924 (he pitched and won both ends of a doubleheader against Chicago on September 6, 1924) and then was traded to the Yankees for the 1925 season. He continued to pitch well, compiling a 49-29 record over the next three seasons, and was a part of the memorable 1927 New York team. Shocker appeared in two games in the 1926 World Series against the Cardinals and was charged with one defeat. He did not appear in the 1927 series and early in 1928 was released. Suffering from failing health, he moved to Denver, Colorado, and pitched semi-pro baseball. After a game on August 6 he contracted pneumonia and was admitted to the hospital a week later. Shocker showed signs of recovery, but suddenly relapsed and died. The cause of death was not only pneumonia, but heart disease. His heart had enlarged considerably from the long innings of toil, and this had finally taken its toll.

Other members of the Browns wound up playing for the team that had beaten them by a single game in 1922. Severeid split the 1926 season between Washington and New York, but got to the Yankees in time to catch Shocker in the World Series. He then spent the next ten seasons in the minors, some as a manager and coach. The Iowa native spent 29 years as a player and caught 2,603 games. This is a record believed to be unmatched by any other catcher. He spent the remaining years of his life as a scout with the Cincinnati Reds, Chicago Cubs, and Boston Red Sox. Severeid's catching companion at St. Louis, Pat Collins, joined the Yankees in 1926 and stayed through 1928. He was one of the three catchers who split the work with the 1927 team, though Collins appeared in more games than either Benny Bengough or Pat Grabowski. Cedric Durst also played for the 1927 Yankees, but is better remembered as the successful fill-in for Earl Combs in the 1928 series. Combs was injured and limited to pinch-hitting roles, and Durst, as well as Ben Pascal to a lesser extent, took his place. Durst played and hit well to include a home run in the fourth game, as New York swept the Cardinals four games to none. Gene Robertson became a regular with the Browns and stayed with them through the 1926 season. After a year in the minors he was with the 1928 Yankees, appearing in the World Series along with Collins and Durst. The latter two also played in the 1927 series.

The only member of the team to become a regular major

league manager other than George Sisler was Marty McManus. The Browns' second baseman was traded to Detroit for the 1927 season and remained with the Tigers through most of 1931. He reached two career highs at Detroit, hitting 18 home runs in 1929 and stealing 23 bases in 1930 for the league leadership. Traded to Boston late in 1931, he was appointed playing manager in June 1932 by Bob Quinn, who was now the president of the Red Sox. The team finished last, but McManus brought them up to seventh in 1933. However, Quinn sold the team to Tom Yawkey that year and McManus was not retained. He ended his major league career with the Boston Braves in 1934. Thereafter he managed in the minors off and on until 1947. He played an early role in the baseball labor movement when he appeared before the executive council of the American Federation of Labor to urge the unionizing of minor league players. McManus reasoned that if that step occurred first then major league players would ultimately fall in line. He died of cancer in a St. Louis hospital February 18, 1966, after working as a house detective in a Chicago hotel.

Other than Jimmy Austin, Johnny Tobin was the only member of the 1922 Browns to subsequently serve as a coach with the team. In 1923 Tobin drove Lee Fohl crazy by bringing a pet monkey on a road trip, and he continued to do the same to American League hitters. Prior to 1926 he was traded to Washington and then on to Boston before the season was complete. Retiring after spending 1927 with the Red Sox, Tobin was engaged in a number of pursuits: sporting goods, sales, fire fighting. In 1949, then Browns president Bill Dewitt signed Tobin as a coach. He served through the 1951 season when the Dewitts sold out to Bill Veech. He was honored with a special night of his own on August 17, 1949 at Sportsman's Park. Tobin passed away in St. Louis on December 10, 1969.

Tobin's two other outfield companions, Jacobson and Williams, also later played in Boston. The three had played in the St. Louis outfield for seven consecutive seasons, 1919 to 1925, and all hit .299 or higher during that time frame. Jacobson joined the Red Sox during the 1926 season and then spent 1927 with Boston,

Cleveland, and Philadelphia. Following two years in the minors he retired after the 1929 season. Before leaving the Browns, Jacobson in 1924 handled 502 total chances (488 put-outs, seven assists, seven errors) a figure that has been exceeded by only two other American League outfielders, Dom DiMaggio and Jim Busby. This mark stood as the major league record until 1928 and American League record until 1948. His fielding percentage for the season was .986, which was naturally good for the league lead. The Illinois native returned to his boyhood Moline area and farmed until his death on January 16, 1977.

The other member of the outfield, Ken Williams, stayed with the Browns until the end of the 1927 season. Then he too moved to Boston for the last two years of his career. While Williams was always regarded as a long ball threat he never came close to the 39 he hit in 1922. His next subsequent best home run year was 1923 when he hit 29. All during his years with the Browns Williams maintained his residence at Grants Pass, Oregon, and it was there he returned once his career was over. Active in fraternal and lodge activities, he ran a billiard parlor in later years until ill health forced him to retire. Williams died in Grants Pass on January 22, 1959.

Gerber also made the "shuffle" to Boston shortly after the 1928 season began. He was the last of the 1922 players to depart and spent the remainder of 1928 and all of the following season with the Red Sox. But before his Browns days were over he handled 48 consecutive chances during four games in 1923. This established a record at the time. After service with St. Paul in the American Association Gerber tried umpiring in the Mid-Atlantic League in the mid–1930s. Ultimately he joined the city recreation department in his hometown of Columbus, Ohio, as a men's activities supervisor. Ill health forced him to retire in 1949 and he passed away June 19, 1951.

The season of 1923 was the last in the major leagues for Eddie Foster, who played such a key role at third base for the Browns for the last month and a half of the 1922 season. Foster retired to the Washington, D.C., area where he had played for the

Senators in earlier years. He operated a metal welding business in the capital. Always very religious, the Chicago native was active in church life and served as a Bible class teacher. On January 7, 1937, he was the victim of a hit-and-run automobile accident and died nine days later of the injuries he sustained.

Another team member who died at a relatively young age (Foster was 50) was Frank "Dixie" Davis, the pitcher of the memorable last game of the September Yankee series. Davis died at 51 on February 5, 1944, in Raleigh, North Carolina, while being taken by ambulance to a hospital. Davis pitched for the Browns until the end of the 1926 season and then later with Kansas City of the American Association. After his baseball career was over he was involved in the tobacco business in Oxford, North Carolina.

The only pitcher to ever truly master Babe Ruth, Hubert "Shucks" Pruett (in 1922 Pruett struck out Ruth 13 times in 16 at-bats), proved to be an otherwise ordinary pitcher. After completing the 1924 season with the Browns Pruett bounced around with the Philadelphia Phillies and New York Giants before ending his career with the Boston Braves in 1932. His career record was 29-48 with an earned run average of 4.63. But Pruett had accomplished what he set out to do: earn enough money through baseball to pay his way through medical school. He became a doctor and practiced in St. Louis thereafter. Once out of the game he proceeded largely to ignore it. Ray Gillespie commented:

> He's rather resentful talking about baseball, sports, and all that sort of thing. All he's concerned about is the medical profession. . . . But I never could understand that except that when he came into baseball he came in with the understanding that he was going to earn his tuition through the medical school at Missouri University. But he stuck around for quite a few years, so I don't know why he is resentful because he's a very fine person, very nice man, not a rowdy or anything like that.

Another 1922 veteran who at first remained in St. Louis was pitcher Bill Bayne. After the 1924 season with the Browns, Bayne dropped to the minors, returning to Cleveland in 1928. He finished with the Red Sox, like a number of the others, pitching there for the 1929 and 1930 seasons. Bayne managed in the minors and then took a civil service job from which he retired in 1970. After a period of prolonged illness he died on May 22, 1981. Pruett followed him in death on January 28, 1982.

Dave Danforth would go to his grave at the age of 80 in 1970 denying that he ever did anything to a baseball that wasn't proper. Danforth was a graduate of Baylor University and the University of Maryland dental school. After leaving the game following the 1932 season he practiced dentistry in the Baltimore, Maryland, area. Danforth's best years with the Browns were 1923 and 1924 when he posted 16-14 and 15-12 records respectively. He finished his baseball career in such minor league stops as Milwaukee, New Orleans, Buffalo, Chattanooga, and Scranton. His 16-4 mark with New Orleans in 1927 helped that team get into the Dixie Series against Wichita Falls. Danforth could not help there as the Texas League champs swept the series four games to none.

Elam Vangilder's 19-13 record with the 1922 team was to be the highlight of his career, but he nonetheless was one of the last to depart the Browns. He pitched for Detroit in 1928 and 1929 to bring his major league career to an end. Vangilder then spent his remaining years farming in the Cape Girardeau, Missouri, area while also serving some time as a local sheriff. When the 1944 Browns made it to the World Series against the Cardinals he trekked to St. Louis to attend game three. He was 81 when he passed away on April 30, 1977.

Jimmy Austin's career with the Browns extended until 1932, giving him more service with the club in the player-coach-manager category than anyone else in the 52-year history of the franchise. After 1922 Austin was exclusively a coach, except for his two-month stint as manager in 1923 and some rare appearances as a player, until the close of the 1932 season. He coached for the White Sox from 1933 to 1940. As late as 1929 at the age of 50 then manager Dan Howley inserted him at third base in a late season game. The old "Pepper Pot" responded by handling two chances cleanly and going zero for one at bat. Austin had long wintered at Laguna Beach, California, and died there on April 6, 1965.

Frank Ellerbe, who contributed so much to this book, played with the Browns in 1923 and then was traded to Cleveland for the 1924 season. After that year "Gov" played a season with Kansas City of the American Association and then retired. Using his baseball earnings Ellerbe settled in Latta, South Carolina, as a cotton and tobacco farmer. Until his late 80s he still fished "about every good day . . . and I can load, unload, and paddle my light boat." The last member of the '22 team died July 8, 1988.

Bob Quinn hired Lee Fohl to manage the Boston Red Sox for 1924, and Fohl stayed there until 1926. That team had nowhere near the talent that the 1922 Browns had had, and the Red Sox rose no higher than seventh during Fohl's three-year tenure. Fohl died in Cleveland on October 30, 1965. Quinn sold the Red Sox to Tom Yawkey in 1933, but soon became involved in the ownership group of the Boston Braves. He served as team president from 1935 to 1945.

The man with the money, team owner Phillip DeCatesby Ball, owned the team until his death in 1933. Only in 1922 did the Browns make money ($350,000) or pose a serious threat to the American League pennant. Nonetheless he continued his interest in the team, seeing it lose considerable money and status in St. Louis as the Cardinals became the city's successful major league entry – particularly after the Cardinals' 1926 National League pennant and World Series victory. And yet there was a time when Cardinal players felt that the Browns were the city's true home team and they were the outcasts. One can only speculate that the Browns might have been the surviving St. Louis major league franchise if Ball had been able to retain Branch Rickey in 1917.

Ball remained a fervent supporter of American League president Ban Johnson and, correspondingly, a foe of Commissioner Landis. He was the only club president to refuse to sign Landis'

***Top*: Four 1922 Browns make the All–St. Louis Team in 1958. Seated: Ken Williams (second from left), George Sisler (third from left). Standing: Johnny Tobin (third from left), Hank Severeid (sixth from left). (Photo courtesy of Dorothy Tobin Brady.) *Bottom*: Greats from different eras: Willie Mays (left), with "Baby Doll" Jacobson at the annual awards dinner of the St. Louis Chapter of the Baseball Writers of America in January, 1971. (Photo courtesy of Carita Jacobson Johnson.)**

initial contract (Quinn signed for the team) in 1920. When he voted to give Landis a pay raise in 1926 it was observed that it was the first time in Landis' six-year tenure that Ball had voted other than against him.

Ball became an early aviation enthusiast, employing his own company plane and later owning the factory which produced Charles Lindbergh's *Spirit of St. Louis.* He was less enthusiastic about another new invention, radio, fighting to prevent broadcasts from major league parks. He was also president and director of a number of other business enterprises.

In September 1933 Ball was vacationing with his wife at their summer cabin at Battle Lake, Minnesota, and complained of illness while fishing. Dr. Robert Hyland, who was still serving as the Browns' team doctor, went to Minnesota and ordered Ball hospitalized. He died in St. Louis' St. Joseph Hospital of septicemia (blood poisoning) on October 22. The Ball estate ran the team until its sale to Donald Barnes in 1936.

It was under Barnes that the 1922 club would have its "last hurrah" as a team. Barnes brought the players back for a reunion and three-inning game with the 1937 Browns on July 16 of that year. At a luncheon prior to the game all present were introduced and many made brief remarks. The September 18 game with the Yankees was rehashed, and George Sisler seemed to reflect the majority opinion in supporting Fohl's decision at that time to relieve Davis because of Elmer Smith. Only Ray Kolp, Hank Severeid, Cedric Durst, and Josh Billings were not present. The first three were still active as players, while Billings was apparently too busy with a new career in motion pictures to attend. Eddie Foster had been killed in an automobile accident the prior January.

In the mini-game Fohl used his standard 1922 lineup with the exception of Austin at third and Collins behind the plate. The players were introduced to the crowd prior to the game and were enthusiastically welcomed home. Davis started and the present team got to him for two runs. Pruett, Meine, Danforth (Yes, Danforth was back to greet Fohl!) all took turns on the mound. The old Browns could not score runs as easily as they had fifteen years previously, and the game ended in a 2–0 defeat.

There would be other celebrations for specific individuals. In January 1958, Sisler, Tobin, Williams, Shocker, and Severeid were chosen to the All–St. Louis All-Star team at first base, right field, left field, pitcher, and catcher respectively. They were honored at a dinner that month and brought back for a parade and ceremonies at Sportsman's Park in August. The impact of the 1922 team can easily be measured when one observes that these players captured one-third of the positions on the 14-man all-star team. Those present were both happy and sad at the August pregame festivities. The *Post-Dispatch* quoted Ken Williams: "This is the greatest honor I've ever had. It's wonderful to be back in St. Louis, a great privilege. Thanks to the fans, the owners, all of you." Six months later he was gone. Hank Severeid: "It's hard for me to take the passing of the Browns and I'm sure many fans have the same feeling. I put in 11 years with the Browns, all happy ones." Pat Collins came from his Kansas City home to be with his former teammates.

What may have been the *very* last hurrah occurred in January 1971. The St. Louis baseball writers awarded their Brian P. Burnes Nostalgia Award to William Chester "Baby Doll" Jacobson. The award was presented at the writers' annual dinner, and Jacobson came in with his son Ted to accept the award. Earlier in the day, two of the three surviving starters on the team–Jacobson and Sisler–held what was to be in effect the last reunion of the team. The meeting was held at Sisler's home with *St. Louis Globe Democrat* sports editor Bob Burnes present. As the conversation drew to a close Burnes reported Sisler asking Jacobson:

> "Any regrets, Jake?"
>
> "No, I don't guess so, George,' responded Jacobson. "I wish I could have played ball more as a boy, but it seemed we were awful busy on the farm. And I guess I'm sorry it ended so soon. Fifteen years. But I wouldn't trade them. A

> lot of memories. Maybe I wish the fellows today would think a little more about us old guys, cut us in for a little bit of pension. It would help . . . but no, I wouldn't change a thing. . . .

Perhaps, if nothing else, this book will at least allow some to think a little more about the old guys.

APPENDIX A

Batting, Pitching, and Fielding Statistics

Batting

	Pos	B	T	G	AB	R	H	2B	3B	HR	RBI	SB	AVG
Austin, James	3B	B	R	15	31	6	9	3	1	0	1	0	.290
Bayne, William	P	L	L	26	30	2	7	0	0	0	3	0	.233
Billings, John	C	R	L	5	7	0	3	1	0	0	2	0	.429
Bronkie, Herman	3B	R	R	23	64	7	18	4	1	0	2	0	.281
Collins, T. Patrick	1B-C	R	R	63	127	14	39	6	0	8	23	0	.307
Danforth, David	P	R	L	20	23	1	2	0	0	0	0	0	.087
Davis, Frank	P	R	R	25	59	4	8	1	0	0	2	0	.136
Durst, Cedric	OF	L	L	15	12	5	4	1	0	0	0	0	.333
Foster, Edward	3B	R	R	85	253	40	67	7	0	0	15	4	.265
Gerber, Walter	SS	R	R	153	604	81	161	22	8	1	51	6	.267
Henry, Frank	P	R	L	4	0	0	0	0	0	0	0	0	.000
Jacobson, William	OF	R	R	145	555	88	176	22	16	9	102	19	.317
Kolp, Raymond	P	R	R	32	57	7	17	6	1	0	6	0	.298
McManus, Martin	2B	R	R	154	606	88	189	34	11	11	109	9	.312
Meine, Henry	P	R	R	1	1	0	0	0	0	0	0	0	.000
Pruett, Herbert	P	L	L	30	34	1	5	1	0	0	1	0	.148
Severeid, Henry	C	R	R	137	517	49	166	32	7	3	78	1	.321
Shocker, Urban	P	R	R	48	115	14	22	3	1	1	6	1	.191
Shorten, Charles	OF	L	R	55	131	22	36	12	5	2	16	0	.275
Sisler, George	1B	L	L	142	586	134	246	42	18	8	105	51	.420
Tobin, John	OF	L	L	146	625	122	207	34	8	13	66	7	.331
Vangilder, Elam	P	L	R	45	93	16	32	10	2	2	11	0	.344
William, Kenneth	OF	L	R	153	585	128	194	34	11	39	155	37	.332
Wright, Wayne	P	R	R	31	50	6	7	2	0	0	1	0	.140

Pitching

	G	IP	H	BB	SO	CG	SO	W	L	PCT	ERA
Bayne, William	26	93	86	37	38	3	0	4	5	.444	4.55
Danforth, David	20	80	93	38	48	3	0	5	2	.714	3.27
Davis, Frank	25	174	162	87	65	7	2	11	6	.647	4.09
Henry, Frank	4	5	12	5	1	0	0	0	0	.000	14.40
Kolp, Raymond	39	170	199	36	54	9	1	14	4	.778	3.92
Meine, Henry	1	4	5	2	0	0	0	0	0	.000	4.50
Pruett, Herbert	39	120	99	59	70	4	0	7	7	.500	2.32
Shocker, Urban	48	348	365	57	149	29	2	24	17	.585	2.97
Vangilder, Elam	43	245	248	48	63	19	3	19	13	.594	3.42

Club Batting	G	AB	R	H	2B	3B	HR	RBI	SB	PCT	
	154	5416	867	1693	291	94	97	781	132	.313	1st Place

Club Fielding	G	PO	A	E	DP	PCT	
	154	4168	1880	201	158	.968	6th Place

APPENDIX B

Dave Danforth Statement, St. Louis Post-Dispatch August 13, 1922

This is the first time I have ever told how I throw a ball. I do not do anything illegal, anything outside the law of pitching, but in the past I always have thought that what I did was my own business, so long as it was honest, and so I always have refused to divulge my method of holding a ball, etc.

Now, that I am about to be railroaded to the minor leagues, I want to make a statement before a notary public or on a stack of Bibles.

I not only did not put mud in the seams of that ball that Umpire Owens found in that game July 27, but I never put mud or dirt in the seams of any baseball. When I was experimenting with freak pitching in the days when such deliveries were allowed I did try loading seams in the bull pen. But that apparently had no effect on the ball and I never have pitched a ball in a game in my life with loaded seams.

My secret is this: I take a baseball after it is thrown to me by the umpire and run my hands, usually moist, over one side of the ball. That is the sum total of my special treatment. Every pitcher in baseball rubs the ball with his hands. Why? Because that makes the ball smooth and gives the pitcher a better grip on the ball with his fingers.

On every baseball, even those fresh from the box, you will find fuzzy spots on the surface and along the seams. Balls which have been used for some time are rougher, the fuzziness is more pronounced. Now when I rub one side I smooth the surface of this fuzz on one side and not on the other.

I don't know that that makes the ball hop or sail. But it certainly is within the law. The rule that permits the pitcher to rub the ball does not specify that he must rub all the way around, that he must be particular to get every bit of gloss removed. Watch any ball game and you will see the pitcher pat his hand in the dust and then rub the ball. Did I ever pat my hand in the dust? No, because I had been advertised all over the circuit as a cheater and every time I pitched the umpires and players were looking for something to kick about.

I always rubbed the ball the same way for every pitch and always held the ball the same way, with the smoothed side up. If I found an uneven spot on a ball I never tried to take advantage of it. I would call an umpire's attention and throw it out. My great misfortune was that I did not notice the dirt on that ball that Owens threw out. I guess it made little difference, though. If they were watching me that way they would find some circumstantial evidence some day and that's all they waited for.

I went to Lee Fohl and told him I did nothing more than other pitchers, but he gave me no sympathy. The umpire had put me out and I had no one to fight for me. I asked Fohl to let me pitch and that I would even give up that rub that I had given the ball so long. But he said "no chance," that I was through. I spoke to Quinn and he referred me to Fohl. I am surprised that all the big league clubs waived on me.

If there is anything illegal in rubbing the hands on the ball, on one side or all sides, then I am guilty of illegal pitching and every other pitcher in baseball is equally guilty. But I never have rubbed dirt or any foreign substance on the ball and I never loaded a seam.

To put me out of the big leagues because an apparently doctored ball was found in the game appears to me to be rank injustice. I know I cannot change the situation, but I want the public to know that I plead not guilty.

Ever since I joined the Browns I have been subjected to continual nagging by the umpires, all because of adverse publicity. Umpire Moriarity came out to me in Washington and said, "I know you, Danforth. You've got some white powder hid about you somewhere."

I felt like laughing in his face, but I knew that would anger him.

Other umpires decided I must be loading the seams and every time a bit of dirt was found in the seams, I had done it. How can pitchers rub a ball with their dirty, sweaty hands without rubbing some dirt into the seams?

Then the umpires nagged me about my motion to first. One said I didn't step to first. Another said I had a swinging step that was illegal. Another said I stepped, but raised my foot too high, and the whole trouble was that I had perfected a legal motion that would fool the best of base stealers. That didn't look right and so umpires decided I must be doing something wrong.

But I gave up that motion and I was ready to give up my pitching secret, but because an umpire decided I was guilty I am kicked out of the league without a hearing or another chance. Umpire Owens said finding the ball did not indicate that I was guilty, but the specific rule called for my expulsion. And so without even having been charged with anything I am thrown out of the league. It certainly doesn't appear fair to thus brand me as an unfair pitcher. I can't try to beat back. If I show any good form no one will pay any attention to it. They'll remember that I was up before, that I am no longer a youngster and it'll be a tough row to hoe.

APPENDIX C

The "Little World Series" Games

Game One, Saturday, September 16, 1922

Browns

	AB	R	H	PO	A	E
Tobin rf	4	0	1	1	0	0
Foster 3b	4	0	1	1	1	0
Sisler 1b	4	0	1	7	1	0
Williams lf	4	0	1	2	0	0
Jacobson cf	3	0	1	3	0	1
McManus 2b	3	0	0	2	3	0
Severeid c	3	0	1	10	1	0
Gerber ss	2	1	1	0	0	0
Shocker p	3	0	0	1	1	0
	30	1	7	27	7	1

New York

	AB	R	H	PO	A	E
Witt cf	4	0	1	4	0	0
Smith rf	0	0	0	1	0	0
Dugan 3b	4	1	1	1	2	0
Ruth lf	4	0	1	1	0	0
Pipp 1b	2	0	1	11	0	0
Schang c	4	0	0	5	1	0
Meusel rf-cf	3	1	3	1	0	0
Ward 3b	3	0	0	2	2	0
Scott ss	4	0	2	1	4	0
Shawkey p	4	0	0	0	3	0
	32	2	9	27	12	0

New York 0 1 1 0 0 0 0 0 0 - 2
Browns 0 0 0 0 0 1 0 0 0 - 1

Two base hits - Jacobson, Sisler, Meusel. Sacrifice hits - Ward, Pipp, Gerber. Double plays - Dugan to Pipp, Ward to Scott to Pipp, Severeid to McManus. Base on Balls - Off Shocker 2. Struck out - By Shocker 6, By Shawkey 5. Left on bases - Browns 3, New York 7. Umpires - Evans, Dinneen, and Guthrie. Time of game - 2 hours, 2 minutes.

Game Two, Sunday, September 17, 1922

Browns

	AB	R	H	PO	A	E
Tobin rf	4	0	1	0	0	0
Foster 3b	2	1	1	0	3	0
Sisler 1b	3	2	1	7	1	0
Williams lf	4	2	2	3	0	0
Jacobson cf	4	0	1	3	0	0
McManus 2b	4	0	1	0	2	0
Severeid c	4	0	3	9	1	0
Gerber ss	4	0	2	4	4	1
Pruett p	3	0	0	1	0	0
	32	5	12	27	11	1

New York

	AB	R	H	PO	A	E
Witt cf	4	0	1	1	0	0
Dugan 3b	4	0	1	1	1	0
Ruth lf	3	1	2	1	0	0
Pipp 1b	4	0	1	5	1	0
Schang c	4	0	0	6	4	0
Meusel rf	3	0	0	1	0	0
Ward 2b	3	0	0	4	1	0
Scott ss	3	0	0	5	1	0
Hoyt p	2	0	0	0	1	0
Jones p	0	0	0	0	0	0
a McMillan	1	0	0	0	0	0
	31	1	5	24	10	0

New York 0 0 0 0 0 1 0 0 0 - 1
Browns 0 0 0 0 0 3 0 2 X - 5

a Batted for Hoyt in eighth.

Home run - Ruth, Williams. Stolen Base - Williams. Double Play - Severeid and Gerber. Left on bases - New York 4, Browns 6. Bases on balls - Off Hoyt 1, Jones 2, Pruett 1. Struck out - By Hoyt 5, Jones 1, Pruett 8. Hits - Off Hoyt 9 in 7 innings, Jones 3 in 1. Losing pitcher - Hoyt. Umpires - Dinneen, Guthrie, and Evans. Time - 1 hour, 58 minutes.

Game Three, Monday, September 18, 1922

Browns

	AB	R	H	PO	A	E
Tobin rf	4	0	1	2	0	0
Foster 3b	4	0	0	1	3	0
Sisler 1b	4	0	0	10	1	1
Williams lf	4	1	1	2	0	0
Jacobson cf	2	1	1	3	0	0
McManus 2b	3	0	2	2	5	1
Severeid c	1	0	0	4	0	0
Gerber ss	3	0	0	3	2	0
Davis p	2	0	0	0	2	1
Pruett p	0	0	0	0	0	0
Shocker p	0	0	0	0	0	0

New York

	AB	R	H	PO	A	E
Witt cf	4	0	3	0	0	0
Dugan 3b	5	1	1	2	0	0
Ruth lf	4	0	0	4	1	0
Pipp 1b	4	0	1	13	0	0
Meusel rf	4	0	0	0	0	0
Schang c	4	0	1	2	2	0
Ward 2b	2	0	0	2	6	0
a Smith	0	0	0	0	0	0
b McNally 2b	0	1	0	1	1	0
Scott ss	2	1	0	2	4	0
Bush p	4	0	0	4	3	0

New York 0 0 0 0 0 0 0 1 2 - 3
Browns 0 0 0 0 1 0 1 0 0 - 2

a Batted for Ward in ninth.
b Batted for Smith in ninth.

Two base hits - Jacobson, Williams, Dugan, McManus. Sacrifices - Davis, Scott,

Severeid, Jacobson, McNally. Double plays - Ruth, Schang, Ward, and Pipp; Foster, McManus, and Sisler. Left on bases - New York 8, St. Louis 3. Bases on balls - Off Bush 1, Davis 2, Pruett 1. Struck out - By Bush 2, Davis 3. Hits - Off Davis 4 in 8 innings (none out in ninth), Pruett 0 in 0 (none out in ninth, two runs in), Shocker 1 in 0. Hit by pitcher - By Bush (Jacobson). Losing pitcher - Pruett. Umpires - Guthrie, Evans, and Dinneen. Time of game - 2 hours, 16 minutes.

BIBLIOGRAPHY

Books

Creamer, Robert. *Babe: The Legend Comes to Life*. New York: Simon & Schuster, 1977.

Lieb, Frederick G. *The Baltimore Orioles: An Informal History of a Great Baseball Club in Baltimore and St. Louis*. New York: Putnam, 1955.

Meany, Tom. *Baseball's Greatest Hitters*. New York: Barnes, 1950.

________. *Baseball's Greatest Teams*. New York: Barnes, 1949.

________ *The Yankee Story*. New York: Dutton, 1960.

Ritter, Lawrence S. *The Glory of Their Times*. New York: Macmillan, 1966.

Ruth, Babe, with Bob Considine. *The Babe Ruth Story*. New York: Scholastic, 1974.

Smelser, Marshall. *The Life That Ruth Built: A Biography*. New York: Quadrangle/New York Times, 1975.

Smith, Robert. *Babe Ruth's America*. New York: Crowell, 1974.

Sobol, Ken. *Babe Ruth and the American Dream*. New York: Ballantine, 1974.

Wallop, Douglas. *Baseball: An Informal History*. New York: Norton, 1969.

Newspapers

Florence (S.C.) *Morning News*

New York Daily News

New York Times

Rock Island (Ill.) *Argus*

St. Louis Globe Democrat

St. Louis Post-Dispatch

St. Louis Star Times

Sporting News

INDEX